A GUIDE TO THE INDUSTRIAL ARCHAEOLOGY OF WILTSHIRE

Edited by M. C. Corfield

PUBLISHED BY
WILTSHIRE COUNTY COUNCIL
LIBRARY & MUSEUM SERVICE
FOR
WILTSHIRE ARCHAEOLOGICAL
& NATURAL HISTORY SOCIETY
1978

Acknowledgements

I would like to acknowledge the help given in the production of this guide. In particular, my thanks go to the individual contributors and to Douglas McKerlie who not only drew the maps but gave great assistance to me in checking drafts and map references. I should also like to thank my colleagues in the Library & Museum Service, the staff of the museum at Devizes who have all given helpful advice, and Miss Jane Butterworth for her help in compiling the bibliography.

M. C. CORFIELD

Sites

The inclusion of sites in this guide does not imply that access is permitted to the public, and in all cases, unless the site is public, the owner's permission should be sought. Sites of especial interest are listed at the end of each section.

Illustrations

Maps are drawn by Douglas McKerlie; photographs, except where otherwise acknowledged, are by the editor.

Metrication

In deference to the present generation in schools who are not being taught the imperial system of measurement, most dimensions in this guide have been converted to the nearest metric equivalent. Generally, imperial dimensions have been given in brackets, but exceptions occur when a structure was constructed to a normally accepted imperial measure, for example, rail and canal gauges. Maps are to the new metric scale with 10 km grid squares.

Published by Wiltshire County Council Library & Museum Service
Bythesea Road, Trowbridge, Wiltshire
for
Wiltshire Archaeological & Natural History Society
The Museum, 41 Long Street, Devizes, Wiltshire

ISBN 0 86080 008 3
Printed in Great Britain
by Dawson & Goodall Ltd., The Mendip Press, Bath
First published 1978

CONTENTS

Maps

Illustrations

INTRODUCTION

In 1970 the first guide to the industries of Wiltshire was published by the Wiltshire Archaeological and Natural History Society under the editorship of Mr. Kenneth Ponting. The interest shown in the guide has encouraged the Society to publish a new, expanded version in which more of the background to the industries can be provided.

Naturally, despite the increase in the information contained in this book there is much which is not included and new information is constantly coming to light. Many of the industries have been the subject of detailed studies and the results published separately; other industries would warrant such study.

The study of industrial archaeology is far more than the recording of the physical remains of past activity; of equal importance are the records of the companies, the reasons for their emergence, their success and finally the reasons for their decline. Sadly, few business records have been preserved. However, those of J. & T. Clark and G. N. Haden are notable survivors, now in the County Record Office.

Wiltshire has many advantages for the student of industrial archaeology. Straddling the routes between London and the west, the county has been traversed by successive routes from east to west and numerous lesser routes from north to south. The imprint of the leading civil engineers of their day is to be seen, Rennie and Whitworth, outstanding canal engineers, Macadam the road builder, and Brunel and Locke, railway engineers *par excellence*. More recently the M4 has cut its swath across the county, bringing with it new transport, unfettered by canal bank or rail track, making areas of the county not served by earlier means attractive to industry.

Many of the traditional manufacturing industries have declined; the textile industry, once the mainstay of the county, is now reduced to a solitary firm: many of the former mills and workshops have been adapted by newer industries, notably the rubber industry in Bradford-on-Avon and Melksham. A few have been lost.

Although never a major source of industrial raw materials, Wiltshire sustained a useful iron industry for sixty years at Westbury: a less successful venture at Seend lurched from crisis to crisis for thirty years. In the production of building materials the county was self-sufficient, the great variety of the geology being reflected in the range of architectural materials; the great stone quarries at Box and Corsham had a fame far beyond Wiltshire's border.

The inventive genius of Wiltshire's engineers can be seen in the work of men such as Job Wastfield of Bradford-on-Avon, and John Fowler of Melksham. Engineers who made their names in Wiltshire include George Haden, millwright, steam engine maker and pioneer of central heating.

No résumé of the industries of Wiltshire would be complete without mention of agriculture. The contribution of agriculture to the development of the industries of the county is inestimable; sheep on the downs, essential as a source of nutrients to the soil, yielded their wool which led to the development of the woollen industry of the county. Pig and cattle rearing in the north-east gave rise to the industries of food production, leather manufacture and gloving. Over all, it was the engineers who mechanised the factories and farms, enabling them to maintain their productiom in the face of increased demand.

Much of our industrial heritage has been lost, mills have been closed with no record of their contents, which have often been sold for scrap; the buildings have been demolished with little record. Watermills are converted to dwellings, their wooden machinery burned and metal scrapped, leaving a desirable but hollow shell beside a mill leet. Vigilance is needed to ensure that surviving monuments are, if not preserved, which many on architectural and historic grounds deserve, at least recorded should demolition become inevitable. A change in attitude is required, leading to an awareness of the importance of the industrial monument in rural and urban environment.

1. TRANSPORT

1a. Roads

Wiltshire has some of the oldest roads in Britain. Many ancient tracks criss-cross the county, focusing particularly on the centres of prehistoric culture on the Marlborough Downs and Salisbury Plain. Typical routes are the Great Ridgeway and the Harrow Way. Most of the green roads and public rights-of-way and their routes have been well-traced and described.

The pattern of Roman roads within the county is also well known and their routes can be identified on modern 1:50,000 Ordnance Survey maps. Roads from military centres like Cunetio (Mildenhall) and Sorviodunum (Old Sarum) fanned out to link with routes to Winchester, Silchester, Cirencester, Bath and Dorchester. They carried military traffic, but most no doubt also served an economic purpose, like the east-west route through Old Sarum, bringing Mendip lead to the Southampton area. Little is known of the local tracks linking the Roman roads or of the development of the system. Occasionally sections appear where present-day roads follow the same route, and road-works recently on the A354 (Salisbury-Blandford) revealed surfaces down to the Roman level.

The Saxons continued to use both Roman and prehistoric routes, but as their valley settlements increased, there grew up a series of valley roads linking the new centres, and the older routes were abandoned in many areas. In South Wiltshire parallel routes on either side of the valleys are a particular feature as villages grew on both sides.

Medieval and Tudor times brought the development of main 'King's Highways' through the county, linking London, Oxford and Winchester to Bath, Bristol and the South West. Vehicular traffic was limited to slow, cumbersome waggons or heavy carriages for the nobility and royalty, but most routes were only really passable on horseback. Even the roads in towns were poorly maintained and often obstructed by "animals or great heaps of soyle and roobidge (rubbish)" as in Marlborough in the 16th century. The roads in the South Wiltshire chalklands were infinitely better than those over the claylands in North Wiltshire for obvious reasons.

Many tracks were named after their use for market produce e.g. Maltway, Sheepdrove, Oxdrove, Chapmans Way.

Fairs and markets in Wiltshire attracted goods from far afield—fish from Poole, pigs from Wales and cheese from Somerset.

Medieval bridges were simple at first—as the existing pack-horse bridges of the 13th century at Coombe Bissett and Castle Combe. Salisbury grew as a commerce centre as the result of Bishop Bingham's old Harnham Bridge (1224) and ancient Milford Mill Bridge—both still used by traffic.

Maud Heath's causeway near Chippenhan is a reminder of the problems even pedestrians had in getting to market in 1474. (There is another medieval causeway at Lacock.)

The enclosure movement brought changes in the pattern. Land was hedged, ditched and boundaries established over open land everywhere in the county, but the road surfaces under the parish maintenance system—or lack of it—remained appalling. Ogilby's road map of 1675 shows seven major routes in the county—Salisbury to Southampton, Salisbury to Oxford via Tidworth and Hungerford, Marlborough to Trowbridge via Devizes, London to Barnstaple via Amesbury and Warminster, Bristol to Oxford via Malmesbury and Swindon, the Bath Road through Marlborough and Chippenham, and the Marlborough to Lechlade road.

The period of turnpike road development began in Wiltshire with the Bath Road (A4) during 1706–1707, and spread rapidly to create a dense network by the 1760s. Of special interest were the rare 'radiating' trusts like those of Devizes and Warminster. During this period was laid down the general pattern of most of the county's present routes. The General Turnpike Acts after 1773 imposed a duty on the Trusts of providing and maintaining guideposts and milestones along their roads. Some 350 milestones and mileposts remain in Wiltshire plus a number of 19th century iron guideposts e.g. near Wardour, at Whaddon and one on Salisbury Plain.

Many milestones were removed during World War II and unfortunately lost. A few are still being discovered where buried as hedgerows are removed e.g. near Chitterne. (Robert Haynes of the Wiltshire Department of Architectural Services has made a full survey of Wiltshire milestones.)

It is reputed that the large cast-iron pumps which were located in places along the A4 between Staines (Middlesex) and Bath were erected to lay dust, and for the comfort of coach passengers, at two mile intervals and at Beau Nash's expense in 1754. Several remain, but the Savernake one was damaged and is being restored.

Road surfacing, following the ideas of Telford and Macadam, was carried out on many of the main turnpikes, indeed Macadam himself was reputedly employed at Devizes, Salisbury and Warminster. Other roads were little improved over the chalk or gravel tracks which existed before, and roads on the North Wiltshire clay continued to be notorious. The last Wiltshire road to be turnpiked was in 1840. The old Salisbury–Devizes turnpike over the military area on the Plain from the Bustard Inn to Redhorn Hill has been tarmac surfaced by the Ministry of Defence, but a section in the target area remains as it was in the early days, though improved with gravel. The improved routes led to a wider development of mail coach services on the main roads, the London–Salisbury coach, for example, averaged 7.4 m.p.h. in 1771, but 9.6 m.p.h. in 1836, whilst the speed of the London–Devizes coach was similarly improved. Steam transport appeared in the mid-1850s. As a result, the 1861 Locomotive Act signs restricting weight appeared on many bridges (e.g. R. Wylye at North Street, Wilton) and, later, diamond versions on railways and canal bridges, e.g. at Devizes and Bradford-on-Avon. Local carriers' services increased with eight providing 'horse-bus' services into Salisbury each day by the end of the century.

The reconstruction and surfacing of the main roads in the county began in the late 19th and early 20th centuries when steam and motor traffic appeared. The dusty chalk tracks over the downlands were replaced by tarred roads sprinkled with chippings, the old surface often dug out entirely and a new 'Telfordised' stone base laid. Steam rollers, tar boilers and barrels, roadmen's braziers and huts on iron wheels—all the equipment of the early repair gangs of the County Council—became a familiar sight. (One such restored roadman's hut now rests by Wilton Windmill for the use of the custodians.)

Motor vehicles themselves were never made in Wiltshire on a large scale, but the widespread effect of those made by the Scout Motor Company in Salisbury from 1902–1921 is particularly important since their buses and lorries had a great social impact on communications in the villages on the Plain and elsewhere.

The Motor Acts brought the introduction of road signs whilst the RAC and AA motorists' organisations added their distinctive additions to country roads and villages with village name plates and warning signs which still exist at Brixton Deverill, Shrewton (B3086) and elsewhere. Most of these have now been removed as the result of the modern changeover since 1965, but various examples have been preserved by the author. Changes due to Army activities are outlined in the Victoria County History.

Heavier and faster traffic and a vast increase in the number of vehicles have affected Wiltshire's roads as elsewhere and changes by the authorities to keep pace are evident. The annual County Surveyor's Reports detail these, often with photographs of 'before-and-after', which are a valuable record. Many an inn, tollhouse or milestone now stands in a layby on an older section of the route as a solitary reminder of the past. Some milestones have been repositioned at various times as at Dinton (Green) or Amesbury By-Pass (A303). Some tollhouses (e.g. Codford and Devizes) are threatened by heavy road traffic on major routes.

A completely new pattern of major routes and dual-carriageways has begun to develop, and the older relics of a more leisurely age will vanish. The massive 1976 intersection of the A36 and the A303 at Wylye is a foretaste of the future as new routes appear. The M4 carving its way through North Wiltshire has created a welcome peace in Calne and Marlborough just as the A303 By-Pass (along the line of the ancient Harrow Way) has done for Amesbury. This has in some ways reduced the immediate demolition danger to old bridges (like the old stone Queensberry Bridge at Amesbury), and other roadside relics on the old route at the expense of the closure of many old-established inns and garages which no longer have an economic trade as in Wylye and Mere on the old London-Exeter road. (The 'King's Arms' at Calne recalls an earlier change in its coaching notice.)

There are many examples of road furniture—old stone mounting blocks outside inns, iron bollards, pavement footscrapers, letter boxes, streetname plates etc. in most Wiltshire towns especially Chippenham, Corsham, Malmesbury, Devizes, Marlborough and Salisbury. The iron streetname plates in Malmesbury are particularly fine, while Salisbury also has a selection. There are no really rare early P.O. boxes in Wiltshire but V.R. boxes are not uncommon e.g. Salisbury (Meadow Road) and Devizes (Brittox).

A cast-iron oil-lamp standard exists in Salisbury Road, Shrewton, whilst oil-lamp brackets can be found in Malmesbury, Salisbury (The Friary) and opposite the George Hotel in Amesbury as well as elsewhere. Gas-lamp standards have been re-used and adapted in several towns.

Road surfaces of earlier types have largely been covered by modern materials; earlier examples (e.g. cobbles in Marlborough) have been removed. Road works occasionally give opportunities to observe sections of earlier road foundations. East Knoyle street is one of the rare examples of minor concrete road, laid thirty years ago for military traffic, but now covered with tarmac. Iron rails form kerbs in Shrewton to resist tank damage, whilst at the junction of Fargo Road and Wells Road in Larkhill is a rare example of brick road, laid as an experiment fifty years ago and still sound. It is hoped it will not be covered over with tarmac.

There is still much to be discovered and explored on Wiltshire highways, both documentary and in the field—and much to be preserved. The cast-iron, early 19th century 'Turnpike/County Bridge' plates at St. Thomas' Bridge, Salisbury (A30) deserve better consideration for example, as do some of the similar parish boundary plates on the A36 at Knook and Warminster, etc. It is to be hoped the road authorities will co-operate fully in the preservation of roadside relics and in keeping industrial archaeologists in touch with changes worth recording. It also helps to make a car journey more interesting!

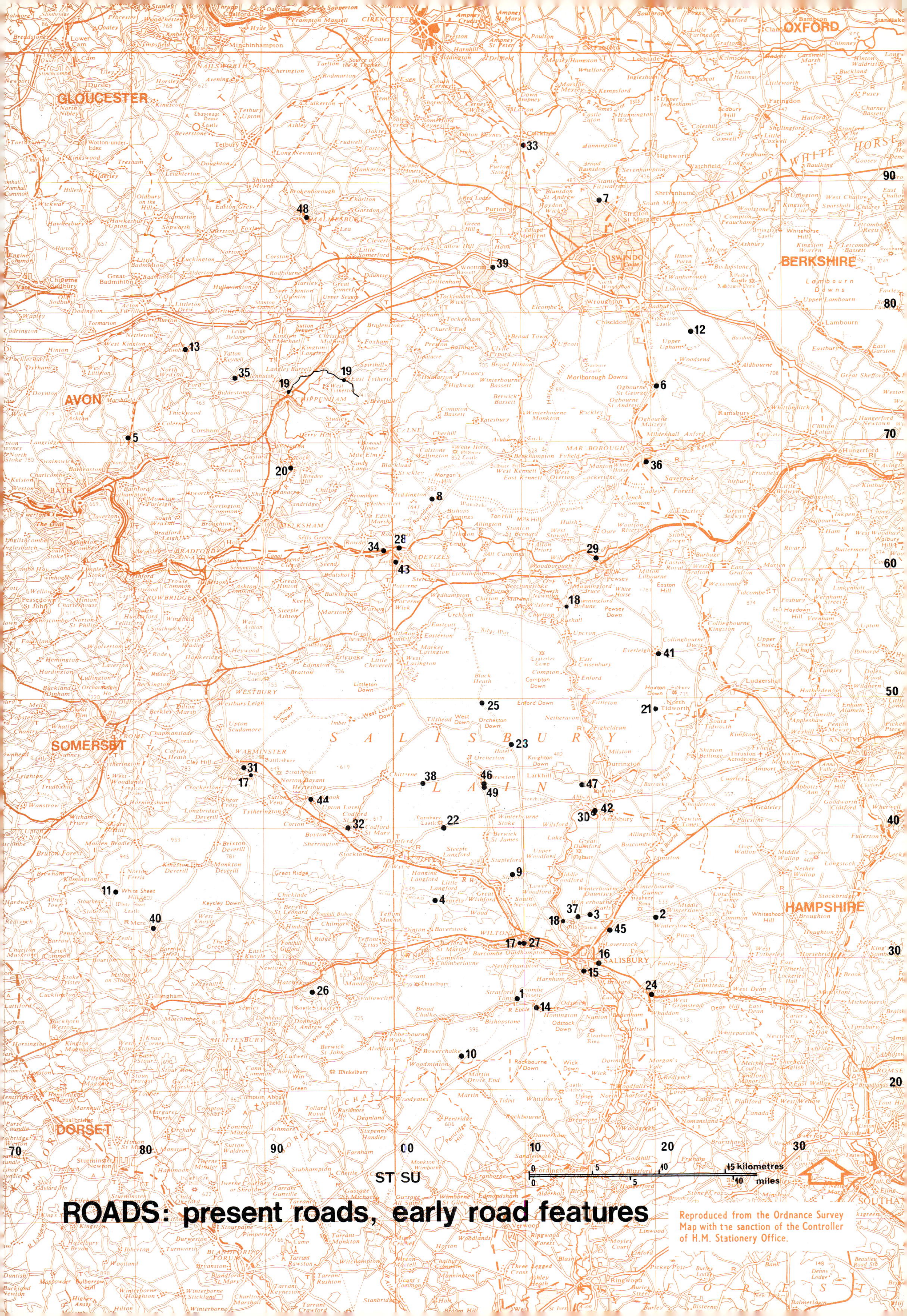

ROADS: present roads, early road features

Reproduced from the Ordnance Survey Map with the sanction of the Controller of H.M. Stationery Office.

Gazetteer

Roman Roads
1. Stratford Tony
2. Winterslow
3. Portway
4. Grovely
5. Fosse Way
6. Ogbourne
7. Stratton St. Margaret

Medieval and Drove Roads
8. Herepath
9. Chain Drove
10. Oxdrove
11. Long Lane
12. Shuger Waie

Packhorse and Medieval Bridges
13. Castle Combe
14. Coombe Bissett
15. Harnham
16. Milford

Parallel Roads
17. Wylye Valley
18. Avon Valley

Causeways
19. Maud Heath's
20. Lacock

Turnpike Roads
21. Old Marlborough Road
22. Old Bath Road
23. Salisbury–Devizes Road

Iron Guide Posts
24. Whaddon
25. Old Devizes Road
26. Wardour

1861 Locomotive Act Signs
27. Wilton
28. Wharf Bridge, Devizes
29. Wharf Bridge, Pewsey
30. Queensberry Bridge, Amesbury

Tollhouses
31. Warminster
32. Codford St. Peter
33. Cricklade
34. Devizes
35. Yatton Keynell
36. Marlborough
37. Old Sarum
38. Chitterne
39. Wootton Bassett

Coach Inns
40. The Ship, Mere
41. The Crown, Everleigh
42. The George, Amesbury
43. Devizes—several examples

Turnpike Signs
44. Parish Boundary Signs A36 Wilton–Warminster
45. County Bridge/Turnpike Sign by St. Thomas' Bridge, Salisbury

Miscellaneous
46. Shrewton kerbs
47. Brick road surface
48. Cast-iron street names (Malmesbury)
49. Oil lamp standard

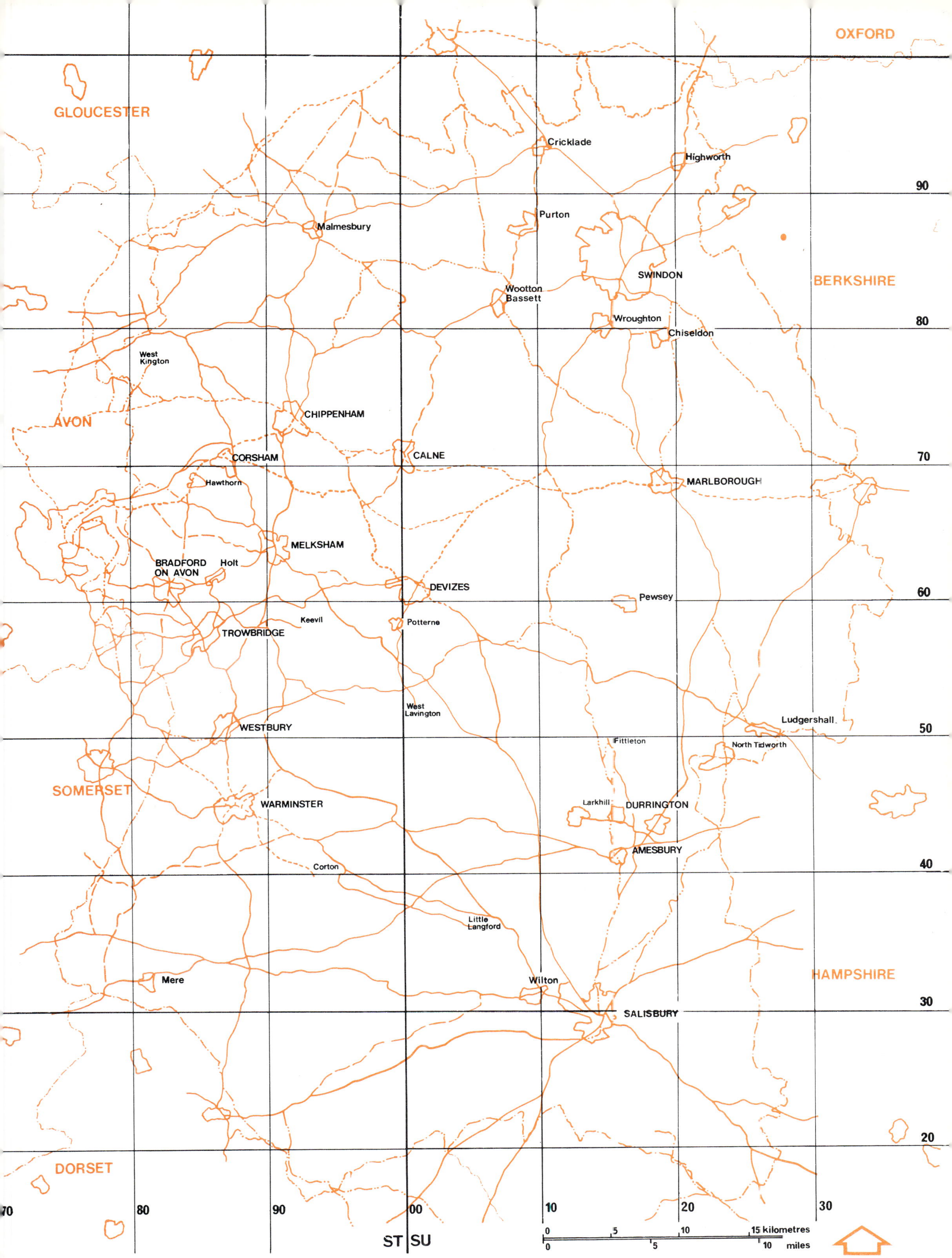

ROADS: development of the turnpike system

roads turnpiked: ----- 1700–1750 —— 1750–1775 — — — 1775–1800 —·· — after 1800

Bromham: Milepost on the Devizes to Chippenham Turnpike. (Photo., Bob Haynes)

Devizes: Shanes Castle, a toll house at the start of the Devizes to Chippenham Turnpike.

Langley Burrell: Maud Heath's Causeway at the River Avon at Kellaways

1b. Canals

From 1761 till the end of the 18th century there was great enthusiasm in Britain for building canals; from 1783 to 1794 it reached such proportions that it is called the Canal Mania. At its peak, in 1792, rumours of the proposals to build a canal from Bristol into Wiltshire prompted an advertisement which appeared in the Salisbury Journal calling a meeting in Devizes to consider its promotion. This advertisement caused the citizens of Bath and Bristol to race to Devizes to attend. This event became known as the 'Ride to Devizes' and was noteworthy enough to be commemorated in two contemporary poems.

In fact, three major projects were finally undertaken in Wiltshire, The Kennet and Avon Canal, the Wilts and Berks Canal and its later extension the North Wilts Canal, and the Southampton and Salisbury Canal Navigation. Of these three, only the Kennet and Avon survives as a navigation and has the most to offer to visitors.

The Kennet and Avon Canal

The first proposal to join the Bristol Avon with the Thames had been made in 1626; the Avon had been navigable from the Severn to Bath since 1727 and the Kennet from Reading to Newbury from 1728. In 1789 Robert Whitworth advised a line via Hungerford, Marlborough and Calne to join Bath to Newbury. However, shortly after, in 1793, John Rennie re-surveyed the route, recommending a more southerly line through Devizes with branches to Marlborough, Calne and Chippenham. Later negotiations with the promoters of the Wilts and Berks Canal allowed that company to serve Calne and Chippenham, while the Marlborough branch was dropped. It was also decided to build a broad canal instead of a narrow one.

Construction began in 1794 and by 1807 the canal was open apart from the Caen Hill Locks at Devizes; Foxhanger and Devizes being connected by tramway. It was opened for through-traffic in 1810 and provided the first direct route by water from Bristol to London, and was also the first through-route to be built as a broad canal. The route passes through Bradford-on-Avon, before which the Avon Valley is twice crossed on the Dundas and the Avoncliff Aqueducts, then close to Trowbridge, through Devizes and the Vale of Pewsey, passing to the north of Pewsey and well south of Marlborough, thence through the Bedwyns, leaving the county at Froxfield.

There were connections with the Somerset Coal Canal at Limpley Stoke, and with the Wilts and Berks Canal at Semington. From the Wilts and Berks there was access to the upper Thames at Abingdon, and by a later branch of that canal, the North Wilts Canal, to the Thames and Severn Canal at Latton Wharf. By these canals through routes to the Midlands were made via the Oxford Canal or the River Severn.

The canal was designed and built by John Rennie, one of the great civil engineers of his time. The pleasing proportions of his bridges and aqueducts together with the lock cottages and offices give the canal an architectural unity lacking in earlier works and add to the pleasure of visiting the attractive countryside through which the canal makes its way.

Rennie had to solve the problem common to most canals, that of providing enough water at the summit where it is least likely to be available to feed the lower levels. This he achieved by taking his summit level through Bruce Tunnel which was only 40 feet above the natural lake of Wilton Water. Above the lake at Crofton he installed two Boulton and Watt beam pumping engines to raise the water to the summit. Additional reservoirs of water were created by making the summit pound two feet deeper than the remainder, and at Wilcot Manor by widening the canal to form a large ornamental lake; this said to be at the insistence of the landowner, Lady Wroughton, who would only sell her land subject to landscaping and the building of the ornamental 'Ladies Bridge'.

At Devizes, where the canal descends into the Avon Valley, the descent is so steep, and the locks so close together, that the pounds have been widened to provide additional supplies of water to prevent the intervening stretches being drained when the locks are filled. On the seventeen locks of Caen Hill itself the pounds are in the form of large rectangular side ponds.

The heyday of the canal was short, since from 1841 the Great Western Railway provided a much quicker and more reliable alternative. The proprietors of the Kennet and Avon struggled to compete with the railway but in 1852 were forced to sell to the Great Western Railway who continued to operate the canal until 1948 when the railways were nationalised and control passed to the Railway Executive. In 1949 the canal was transferred to the Docks and Inland Waterways Executive of the British Transport Commission, which was in turn succeeded by British Transport Waterways and the British Waterways Board, the latter now having overall responsibility for the canal. After years of neglect the canal is being restored to navigation by the combined efforts of the Kennet and Avon Canal Trust and the British Waterways Board. At the time of writing a major obstacle, the fissured section between Dundas and Avoncliff, is being lined to make a sound bed.

Dundas Aqueduct (ST 786 626)

The canal enters Wiltshire from Bath near Limpley Stoke, crossing the River Avon on the fine Dundas Aqueduct 46 m (150 ft) in length. The Somerset Coal Canal joined the Kennet and Avon just before the aqueduct and traces of it can still be seen. There is an iron crane by Acramans of Bristol sited by the aqueduct.

Avoncliff Aqueduct (ST 805 600)

The canal crosses the river by another interesting aqueduct at the canalside hamlet of Avoncliff. Here, as at Dundas, the courses of the tramroads from Conkwell and Murhill quarries can be traced.

Bradford-on-Avon Wharf (ST 825 604)

This wharf served the town of Bradford-on-Avon. On the wharf is a single storey store recently rebuilt with the dry dock alongside covered by a projecting canopy.

Biss Aqueduct (ST 855 594)
A short aqueduct carrying the canal over the River Biss.

Hilperton Wharf (ST 861 602)
This wharf served the town of Trowbridge; most of the buildings associated with it still survive.

Semington Aqueduct (ST 897 609)
A single low profile masonry arch carries the canal over Semington Brook. It has a plaque space and string course, but architecturally is more modest than either Avoncliff or Dundas.

Semington Wharf (ST 899 611)
This wharf stood at the junction with the Wilts and Berks Canal. The blocked off bridge over the entrance to the junction can still be seen. There is a wharfinger's house east of the road bridge, a lock keeper's cottage to the west by the lock, and the Wilts and Berks toll keeper's house facing the road.

Seend (ST 932 613—ST 955 619)
There were four wharves at Seend: Seend, Scott's, Wragg's and Martinslade.

Devizes (ST 968 617—SU 012 617)
Soon after Seend the climb to Devizes begins. There is a total of 29 locks within 4 km (2½ miles), giving a rise of 73 m (237 ft), a flight exceeded only by the 30 locks of the Tardebrigge flight to Birmingham. Of the 29, 17 are grouped together in one impressive flight—Caen Hill; at the top is the B.W.B. maintenance yard and the second of the dry docks on the canal. The toll house is sited alongside lock 45. The canal passes under two bridges with separate towpath arches, the first, Prison Bridge, with a plaque commemorating John Blackwell, Engineer on the canal for 34 years up to 1840; the second, Town Bridge, with an elegant lock keeper's cottage beside it.

There was a number of wharves in Devizes. Sussex Wharf was below Town Bridge, and is commemorated in the name of a small cul-de-sac off The Nursery: the Lower or Stone Wharf was above the Town Bridge, and beyond was Devizes Wharf itself. On the wharf is a warehouse with a hoist to the upper floor facing the canal and an iron crane on the wharf side. Adjacent to the bridge, running away from the canal, is a group of original warehouse buildings.

From Devizes the canal winds through the Vale of Pewsey to Honey Street (SU 103 615), a wharf and canal community. There is a canal inn with its original stabling and various other industrial works which grew around the canal's boat building centre. The history of the site is recorded by a plaque on the works chimney.

Ladies Bridge (SU 129 606)
Built by Rennie in 1808 this is a decorative stone bridge with neo-classical decoration. This elaborate accommodation bridge is unique, such work usually being confined to the major engineering features.

Stowell Park Bridge (SU 145 615)
A mid-nineteenth century suspension bridge built to a Dredge Patent carried a private footpath over the canal.

Pewsey Wharf (SU 158 611)
1 km (⅝ mile) from the town centre the wharf now has a canal house with an adjoining warehouse. North of the canal is the French Horn public house with attached stables.

Bruce Tunnel (SU 236 632)
460 m (1512 ft). The portals are in brick and that at the east end has a memorial plaque to Thomas Bruce, the Earl of Ailesbury, and to Charles, Lord Bruce, his son. Bruce tunnel is notable in that its cross section is exceeded only by that of the Netherton tunnel in Birmingham, which was not built until 1858. There is no towpath, boats were pulled through by hand using chains fixed to the walls.

Crofton (SU 264 624)
3 km (2 miles) from Bruce tunnel, after the canal has started its descent to the east, stands Crofton Pumping Station by the road from Great Bedwyn to East Grafton. The two beam engine pumps are of outstanding interest, one is by Boulton and Watt, the other by Harvey's of Cornwall. A more detailed description is on page 33.

Great Bedwyn (SU 280 645)
A small wharf serving the town. After Great Bedwyn the canal passes through Little Bedwyn and leaves the county at Froxfield.

Along the length of the canal there are many swing bridges, these turn on ball-bearing races and are reputed to be the first use of this device; another frequent survivor is the winch used to open a hatch in the floor of the canal at times when it was necessary to drain a length. At places on the side of the canal the G.W.R. boundary posts can be found.

The Kennet and Avon, though the property of British Waterways Board, is being restored throughout by the combined efforts of the Board and an enthusiastic Trust whose main task is to raise the necessary finance. It also provides volunteer labour where this can be utilised.

The Wilts and Berks Canal
The Wilts and Berks Canal is a very different matter from the Kennet and Avon. Abandoned in 1914 after years of disuse there are few obvious landmarks and little possibility of restoration, though this has recently been suggested. Its fascination lies in the fact that by careful map reading it is possible to trace almost its entire length observing how it was supplied with water, notably from the Rivers Marden and Ray, and from its principal source, Coate Water near Swindon, which was constructed by the Canal Company and is still in use as an amenity.

The canal leaves the Kennet and Avon Canal at Semington (ST 900 601), the only surviving traces being the toll collector's house and the filled-in bridge by which the Kennet and Avon towpath crossed the canal. From here the canal can be traced through

Melksham, with the remains of an embankment and aqueduct over Lowbourne Brook (ST 908 641) and part of an old bridge at the junction of Calne Road and Forest Road. Some wharf buildings remain beside the Devizes Road, as does an unnecessary hump of the former bridge (ST 906 635).

From Melksham the canal proceeds towards Lacock and at ST 914 656 is carried over a stream on an aqueduct; further on the bridge at Queenfield lock is still in use. At Lacock the wharf house survives. From Lacock the course of the canal is traced cutting into the side of Naish Hill overlooking the Avon. At ST 939 713 the Chippenham branch, the entrance to which has been filled in, leaves the main line. The River Marden is crossed by the canal on the Stanley Aqueduct; the collapse of part of one arch here in 1906 caused the closure of the canal. Beyond the aqueduct are the remains of two locks and the junction with the Calne Branch which leaves to the east.

Continuing its course to Swindon, the canal's climb can be seen in the remains of locks at Foxham (ST 981 775), at Dauntsey (ST 995 802) where the lock house survives, and at Wootton Bassett where seven locks lifted the canal up a sharp rise. A house still called 'Seven Locks' is the former lock house. At Tockenham Wick an additional reservoir was built to supply these locks and survives as a trout farm. Vastern Wharf (SU 052 816) is now a timber yard.

At Wharf Farm, and now beside the M4, was Wroughton Wharf; Hay Lane Wharf is commemorated by a house named 'The Wharf'. Approaching Swindon the canal crossed the River Ray in a two-arch aqueduct, and was crossed by a now derelict railway at ST 137 835. In Swindon itself Commercial Road Bridge survives as an elegant balustraded structure. Wharf Road indicates the site of the town wharf. Fleming Way is built over the bed of the canal. The canal is next seen skirting the playing fields beside a surviving footbridge. Outside Swindon the A420 is crossed by the railway on a double-arched, brick bridge. Originally the southern arch was used by the canal, whose level was two metres above the present road level, as indicated by the stone below the brickwork.

The North Wilts Branch has largely been filled in and is best seen in Cricklade, where the south portal of the tunnel survives; and the site of West Mill Wharf by West Mill Lane. At Latton Basin (SU 087 954) the North Wilts had its junction with the Thames and Severn Canal, the stone-lined basin, lock chamber and toll house survive.

The Calne branch is mostly unfilled and can be followed from Calne, where the branch ended at a wharf, now a car park opposite Harris' factory. The Marden flowed in here leaving the canal a short distance away down Station Road, where the remains of the first lock can be seen.

Of the Chippenham branch little remains; the wharf is occupied by the bus station and only one canal house survives.

The Thames and Severn Canal

The Thames and Severn Canal intrudes briefly into Wiltshire between Inglesham (SU 073 972) and Marston Maisey (SU 146 966): on that stretch are two round houses typical of this canal. That at Marston Maisey has the original inverted conical roof designed to catch rainwater for domestic use, while the second, at Cerney Wick (SU 979 961), has a conventional cone. At the Cricklade Wharf is one of the few remaining wharf houses built to the company's design, in which two-storey warehouses flank a central pedimented residence.

The Salisbury Avon Navigation

At the same time that the Kennet and Avon Canal and the Wilts and Berks Canal were being built an ambitious project was launched in the south of the county for a direct canal from Salisbury to the Ocean Wharves at Southampton. This was not the first time that Salisbury had sought a connection with the sea, since in 1664 the River Avon Navigation Act had been passed, which allowed the making of the River Avon navigable from Christchurch to New Sarum and the Wylye to Wilton. This early venture was operated after a fashion but was badly damaged by floods and abandoned in 1730. There are a few traces of this work, the lock at Britford (SU 159 278) is the sole engineering feature surviving. However, some of the channels now used by the water meadow systems may date from the Navigation.

The Southampton and Salisbury Canal Navigation

This venture was even less successful than the Avon Navigation. Begun in 1795, it never reached Salisbury. Poor workmanship, a disastrous flood which destroyed much of the work, and bad management, together with waning interest and chronic lack of money, mainly caused by an expensive scheme to tunnel under the Southampton suburbs, prevented the company getting their canal beyond Alderbury. Some traffic between Dunbridge on the Test and West Grimstead kept the Canal going for a short while until 1808 when all traffic ceased.

Despite its short life, traces of the canal are still to be seen, in particular where it enters the county at West Dean (SU 257 270); here the canal wharf occupies the centre of the village and is an attractive place to visit. By East Grimstead Church (SU 225 272) the only remaining original bridge over the canal survives. At Alderbury the greatest of the canal works survives, this is the deep Alderbury cutting (SU 193 268) excavated on both sides of the saddle but never united by the intended tunnel.

Other Canal Proposals

Many plans for canals were mooted which came to nothing. The chief of these hinged upon the completion of the Salisbury canal; from Salisbury it was proposed that a canal should be cut to a junction with the Kennet and Avon at Wilcot following the Avon Valley, a second canal was to be cut through the Wylye Valley to Warminster. These two canals foundered with the Salisbury canal. A second canal was proposed from the Andover Canal to join the Kennet and Avon at Pewsey. Both canals were to provide an inland route from Bristol to Southampton.

A second north/south route, the Dorset and Somerset

Canal, was to run from near Sturminster Newton to join the Kennet and Avon at Widbrook near Bradford-on-Avon.

One other canal was proposed in Wiltshire, the Bristol Junction Canal which was to run from near Wootton Bassett by way of Malmesbury to Bristol and was intended to give the Wilts and Berks an independent line to that city.

The canals were in their time important feats of civil engineering. They were made at a time of econonic difficulties due to the Napoleonic Wars and presented their builders with severe problems which had to be overcome with the relatively meagre resources then available.

Though their useful life was short, their impact was considerable. The economic benefit to the country through which they passed cannot be over emphasised providing as they did a cheap and swift means of transport for the produce of the land to the hungry towns and cities. The effect of the canals on the towns was as profound. Bath stone transported by canal changed the face of many Wiltshire towns, and as will be seen later, the transportation of coal by canal led to the use of the steam engine in Wiltshire.

East Grimstead:
The last surviving bridge on the short-lived Southampton & Salisbury Canal Navigation

Latton: The basin was the junction of the North Wilts Canal with the Thames & Severn Canal

Marston Maisey: Lock keeper's cottage typical of the Thames & Severn Canal. The roof is an inverted cone to collect rainwater for domestic use

Burbage: The wharf crane, the last survivor of its type on the Kennet and Avon Canal, is being restored by members of the Wiltshire Archaeological Society

Gazetteer

Kennet and Avon Canal

1. Limpley Stoke, Dundas Aqueduct
2. Avoncliff Aqueduct
3. Bradford-on-Avon Wharf
4. Trowbridge, Biss Aqueduct
5. Hilperton Wharf
6. Semington Aqueduct
7. Semington Wharf
8. Seend
9. Devizes
10. Honey Street
11. Woodborough, Ladies Bridge
12. Wilcot, Stowell Park Bridge
13. Pewsey Wharf
14. Burbage, Bruce Tunnel
15. Crofton
16. Great Bedwyn

Wilts and Berks Canal

17. Semington, canal junction and toll collector's house
18. Melksham, Devizes Road, site of bridge and wharf
19. Melksham, Lowbourne, site of aqueduct and bridge
20. Lacock, toll bridge
21. Lacock, Wharf House
22. Chippenham, Stanley Aqueduct
23. Tockenham, Lock House
24. Swindon, aqueduct
25. Swindon, Commercial Road Bridge
26. Swindon, canal bridge
27. Swindon, rail bridge over A420
28. Swindon, Coate Water

North Wilts Canal

29. Cricklade, tunnel portal
30. Cricklade, West Mill Wharf
31. Latton, Canal Basin and junction with Thames and Severn Canal toll house and basin survive

Thames and Severn Canal

32. Cerney Wick, canal lock and cottage
33. Cricklade, wharf and wharfinger's house
34. Marston Maisey, canal bridge and lock cottage

Salisbury Avon Navigation

35. Britford, lock

Southampton and Salisbury Canal Navigation

36. Alderbury, deep cutting
37. East Grimstead, bridge
38. West Dean, course of canal

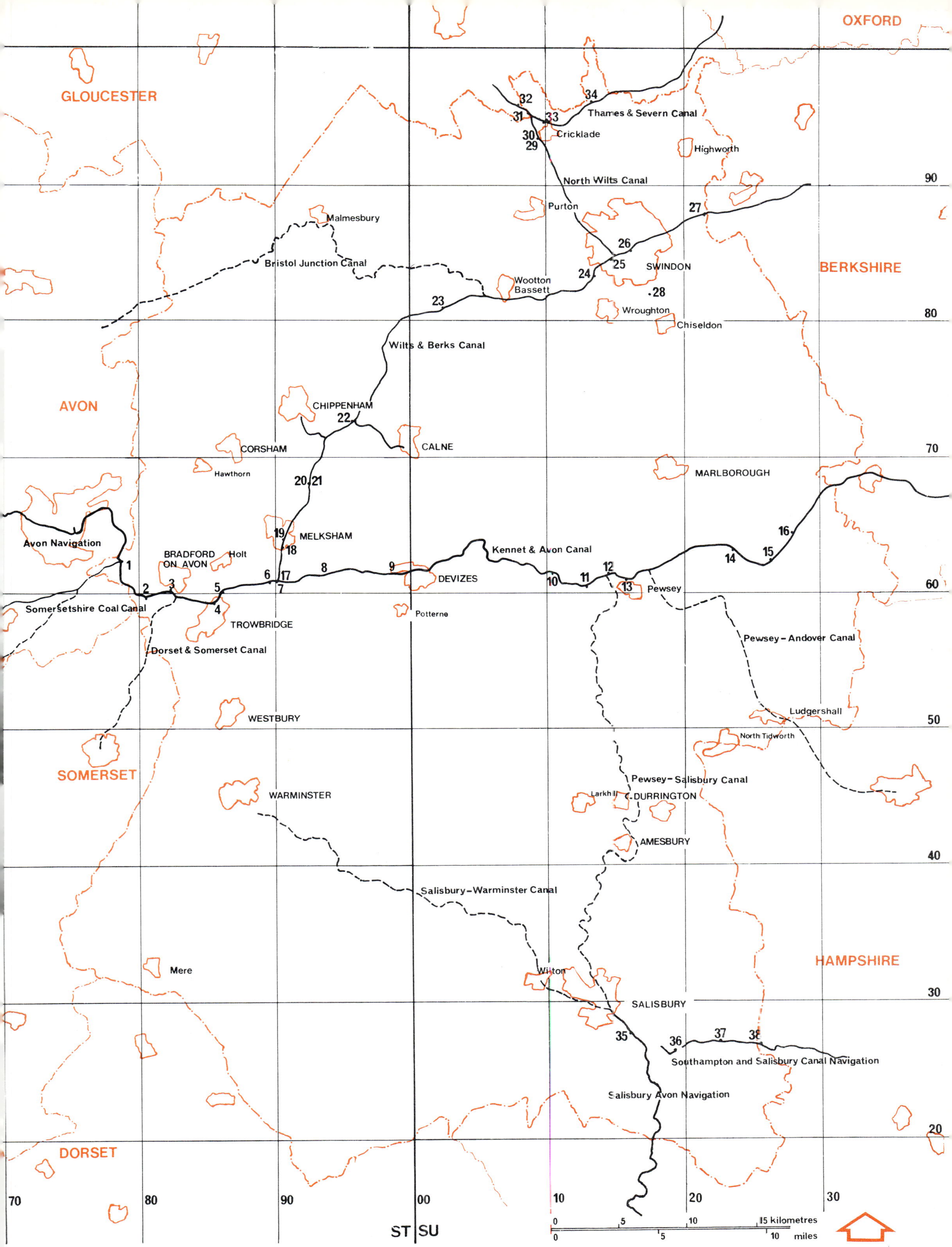

CANALS

broad canal — narrow canal — abortive scheme

1c. Railways

The use of wagons running on rails precedes the accepted 'railway age' of the 19th century by more than two hundred years; a network of wagonways moved coal from the collieries of the north east to the ships of the Tyne in the 17th century. It was natural that similar tramways as these simple railways were called were used as feeders to the canals.

With the availability of cheap iron, thin plates of iron replaced the simple wooden tracks previously used, hence the description platelayers, still used for those men who maintain the modern railway track.

In Wiltshire, during the building of the Kennet and Avon Canal, tramways were laid from the Company's quarries at Conkwell (ST 788 615) and Murhill (ST 796 605). On that at Conkwell the wagons were hauled over a balanced, inclined, plane laid with iron rails; at Murhill the stone was led over a track, having wooden rails secured by spikes set in lead plugs in stone blocks. Neither site survives, but that at Murhill is described by A. P. Voce in the *S. Wilts Industrial Archeology Journal* for 1969. Whilst the great flight of locks was built at Caen Hill, Devizes (ST 976 614), the east and west parts of the canal were linked by a double track tramway constructed with iron rails on wooden sleepers. Some stone block foundations of this tramway survive between lock 45 and lock 28 at Foxhanger.

The birth of the two great railways which were driven from east to west across Wiltshire followed soon after the opening of the first public railway between Stockton and Darlington in 1825. The so-called Bristol Committee, made up of merchants anxious to investigate the possibility of a railway route to London, first met in January 1833, followed in August by a joint meeting of both the Bristol and the London Committees, at which the name Great Western Railway was adopted. Their Act of Parliament received Royal Assent on 31st August 1835.

The promoters of the London and Southampton Railway presented their Bill for a railway between the two cities (instead of a canal as had been first envisaged) and received Royal Assent in 1834.

The Great Western Railway

The Great Western Railway is memorable as one of the great Victorian railways, surviving longer than any other railway company, from 1833 until nationalised in 1947. It achieved a number of successes often identified with the name of the Company's engineer, Isambard Kingdom Brunel.

Unlike many other main lines the G.W.R. did not start as an amalgamation; its main line between Paddington and Bristol was completed in three years after the initial section to Maidenhead (Taplow) was opened in 1841.

Brunel, who had been appointed by the Bristol Committee in 1833, recommended a route north of the Marlborough Downs via Chippenham, Swindon, The Vale of the White Horse and the Thames Valley as it offered easier gradients and gentler curves than did the alternative via Bradford-on-Avon, Devizes, Pewsey and Newbury. It also gave the opportunity for extension to Oxford, Gloucester and South Wales. These circumstances influenced the Parliamentary Committee in favour of the G.W.R. Bill.

Opposition to the Bill came from the London and South Western Railway, who were presenting at this time a Bill for a 'Basing to Bath Railway' to be routed 'through or near Newbury, Devizes, Trowbridge and Bath'. They had to admit that the gradients over this route were generally steeper but in making this admission they added that the gradients were so balanced that the rises and falls compensated for one another so that the line was practically level. This invoked a reply from the Chairman of Committees in Parliament that on this principle the Highlands of Scotland would be as good as any other district for the construction of a railway!

George Stephenson was one of the engineers who gave evidence in favour of the G.W. route (which included the controversial Box Tunnel) as well as Joseph Locke, one of Stephenson's most able pupils.

Ironically, Locke took over the building of the London and Southampton Railway when its first Engineer, Francis Giles, was dismissed. The bitterness during the long Committee stages of these Bills was the beginning of the period of bad relations between the two companies, both seeking to be first to Exeter and the West Country.

In the actual technicalities of railway building, the G.W. from the outset showed an independence of thought, beginning with its rail gauge—the distance between the rails. This had hitherto followed the gauge of the early plateways of the north-east which was 4 ft 8½ in (1.435 m) the distance between the wheels of the chaldron wagons in the Northumberland collieries. This is now generally referred to as the 'standard' gauge but was known as 'narrow' gauge while the broad gauge existed.

Brunel, however, persuaded his Directors there were advantages in having a wider gauge, claiming greater safety and a steadier ride at higher speeds, by permitting a lower centre of gravity on the carriages as with the wide gauge the whole carriage body could be fitted in between the wheels, which in turn could be of a larger diameter. As a result he decided on a rail gauge of 7 ft (2.133 m) and the map shows the routes eventually laid to this 'broad' gauge—by 1852 this extended over the whole of the south-west of England, South Wales and as far north as Wolverhampton.

Where the gauges met, as at Gloucester and Salisbury for example, passengers had to change carriages, and goods were transhipped. The difficulty was later mitigated to some extent by laying a third rail, i.e. a mixed gauge, but this was an unsatisfactory expedient which produced more problems, particularly at points and crossings.

In addition to having a wide gauge Brunel's method of construction of the track differed from that used on the 'narrow' gauge railway—nearly all the broad gauge lines were constructed with flat bottom or 'bridge' rails on heavy longitudinal baulks of timber, supported on piles driven into the ground and held together by cross transomes at relatively long intervals, as illustrated in the view of the west portal of Box Tunnel.

Brunel claimed that this method ensured a more rigid track than the heavy stone blocks which elsewhere supported the rails. There are bits of 'bridge' rail to be seen at quite a few places, although not 'on' track, e.g. being used as fencing approaching the eastern end of Box tunnel, to be seen beside the road that runs alongside the railway.

The Report in 1846 of a Commission appointed to consider the nuisance of the two gauges, virtually ended the extension of the broad gauge as Parliament passed a series of resolutions in favour of the narrow gauge on any *new* railway. At this time there were about 442 km (275 miles) of broad gauge track, out of a total of 3580 km (2225 miles) of railway in Great Britain. The G.W.R. began to acquire narrow or 'standard' gauge lines and made conversions from 'broad' to 'mixed' and standard gauge. The changes accelerated, until, at the end of May 1892, during one weekend, 3400 men, collected from many sources, converted what then remained of the broad gauge—275 km (171 miles) of it! It is still considered by many railway engineers that it was a major tragedy that Brunel's splendid 7 ft gauge, coming as it did in the late 1830s, was too late to become a national, even international, standard.

Returning to 1840—the G.W. main line reached Faringdon Road (now Challow) by 1st June and the next section to be opened, to Hay Lane, three miles west of Swindon, saw the G.W. railway enter Wiltshire in December. At Hay Lane (officially designated Wootton Bassett Road) the railway came within half a mile of the turnpike road, and although simply a temporary 'end of line', it was equipped with sidings and crossing gates which were wide enough to be closed fully across the railway as well as the highway; these because of the recent regulations demanding protection of the public!

Hay Lane (where there is a road bridge over the line now) remained the nearest station for the inhabitants of the little market town of Swindon until sufficient of the new junction station (junction of the main line and the Swindon-Cirencester branch) was ready by the middle of 1841. A new station, refreshment rooms (to be run privately) and workers' cottages (to house the large number of mechanics required for the new Works) were authorised by the Directors only three months after they had approved the building of the workshops. The cottages, together with other amenities i.e. the Hospital and Mechanics Institute, were a far-sighted provision at the time. As a model village it has been renovated with one cottage retained in its original form as an example for visitors. The permanent refreshment rooms and the main block of the new station were opened in July 1842 and consisted of two large, three-storey, stone buildings, one on each side of the lines which were, until the subway was built, connected by a covered bridge. The station has been completely rebuilt in recent years, although the original front is incorporated; it was the only early G.W.R. station of note which did not have a train shed type of overall roof which was typical of Brunel design. Typical of his similar stations are those of Bradford-on-Avon and Chippenham.

Chippenham was reached on 31st May, 1841 and the remaining section of 21 km (13 miles) to Bath was ready for the first through train, of G.W. Directors, from London to Bristol (and Exeter via the Bristol and Exeter Railway) on 30th June, 1841—this last G.W.R. section from Chippenham to Bath included the notorious tunnel under Box Hill. The Bristol–Bath part of the line had been open since 31st August, 1840.

The preliminary work of sinking the trial shafts for Box Tunnel was begun in 1836—the tunnel is straight, slightly less than two miles long and on an incline of 1 in 100 falling towards the western end and accommodates two tracks. At the time it was the longest railway tunnel in the country. In terms of physical effort and suffering, the building of it was a major railway work. The main part of the tunnel was driven through marl, clay and oolite, and needed a brick lining almost throughout its length; a hundred horses and carts spent three years transporting 30 million bricks from a yard near Chippenham. Severe flooding occurred in November 1837 and a year later another inflow halted the work for a time. As the work fell behind timetable Brunel bolstered the work forces until 4000 men and 300 horses were employed. The estimate of £6½ million was finally doubled by the end of the five years of building, in June 1841.

The gradient of 1 in 100 was severe for the engine power of the period, Brunel having in mind the need to concentrate the necessary change in levels into one place, where banking engines could readily be provided. This was a view supported by other eminent engineers when Box Tunnel was being challenged during the presentation of the G.W.R. Bill—Daniel Gooch, the Locomotive Superintendent, in his diary, records that Brunel was anxious about the ability of the locomotive as opening day approached. In the event, no particular problem was experienced. The saga of Box Tunnel, the magnificent west end portal of which can be seen from the adjacent A4 road, cannot be left without a mention of the legend that, on anniversaries of Brunel's birthday (he was born on 9th April 1806 at Portsea) the sun can be seen shining straight through the tunnel. The legend carries conviction from the reply made by the Superintendent of the National Almanac Office of the Royal Greenwich Observatory when his opinion was sought in recent years by Oswald Nock—the rising sun was definitely, in respect of altitude and azimuth, in the position on that date in the year, to make the legend a fact.

Before the Paddington/Bristol line was opened throughout, it was realised that there would be need for a depot or workshops for the repair of engines and rolling stock, in addition to the facilities in the London area. In 1837 Daniel Gooch was appointed Superintendent of Locomotives by Brunel at the age of 20. In 1840 he was instructed by the Directors to report on the most suitable location for such a depot. Gooch reported in favour of Swindon, which in 1840 had a population of about 2500. It was at the junction with the Cheltenham and G.W. Union line, opened as far as Cirencester in May 1841. Gooch's considerations, given at length in his letter dated 13th September 1840 to Brunel, were mainly technical and would discount the story that the site of the Works was chosen by Brunel whilst walking with Gooch in the area, by throwing a half-eaten sandwich over his shoulder with the remark that where it fell would mark the place. The contours of the land had determined the site for the junction with the Cheltenham line and Swindon was at about the right place between Paddington and Bristol to have a repair and maintenance point, as well as being a convenient depot for the Box tunnel banking engines, and a suitable station at which passengers could take refreshments. It was Gooch's intention to use engines with smaller driving wheels for the more heavily graded section between Swindon and Bath and to employ the fast moving locomotives with large driving wheels on the galloping run from Swindon to London.

The Wilts and Berks Canal passed through the town, and was used for the transport of Portland stone from nearby quarries—in Gooch's letter to Brunel, mentioned earlier, Gooch wrote "It (Swindon) has also the advantage of being on the side of the canal communicating with the whole of England, and by which we could get coal and coke, I should think at a moderate price. I am not sufficiently acquainted with the place to know how we would be affected by the want of water, it might probably be collected in the neighbourhood . . . and even if this fail we have the canal". The Canal was used to supply the Works with water in the early days, the siding north of the main station now is known as Water Sidings, no doubt where some sort of tank wagons (spare engine tenders ?) stood.

The new Works were in regular use by January 1843 managed by Archibald Sturrock. They had, under Daniel Gooch, been built largely of the stone excavated from Box Tunnel. The oolite has a pleasing appearance and the grain shows well on many of the original walls which remain today. After trouble with the original locomotives bought from a number of firms, including Rowland Brotherhood of Chippenham, the G.W.R. manufactured its own engines in increasing numbers after 1846 and also, from about 1861, made rails in its own mill at Swindon against considerable opposition from the established Ironmasters.

At its peak 14,000 men were employed in the Works, which is now a third of that size and rationalised to cope with the demands of the diesel/electric railway; but many of the old crafts remain; there are coppersmiths and tinsmiths in No. 3 Shop and patternmakers below the water tower alongside Radbourne Road, a foundry turning out a whole range of non-ferrous castings. It is possible to visit the Works on the well publicised 'Open Days' or on other occasions by prior arrangement with the Works Manager.

Great Western Railway Branches in Wiltshire

The Cheltenham and Great Western Union Railway

The Cheltenham and Great Western Union Railway has been mentioned in connection with the siting of Swindon Works. As early as 1833 a railway from Cheltenham via Gloucester and Stroud to join the line from Bristol was projected by some Cheltenham citizens, but when a Bill was presented in 1836 it was opposed by the London & Birmingham Railway Co. who supported an alternative by bringing a line from Tring to Cheltenham. However, this failed, and the first section of the C. & G.W. Union Railway opened between Swindon Junction, Kemble and Cirencester on 31st May 1841. As far as Kemble, where there was to be a junction between the line to Cirencester and that from Gloucester the line was double, constructed on bridge rails on longitudinal timbers, thus following G.W. practice.

The description of the route when proposed, had a charming ring about it—"from Cheltenham (Cold Bath) and from the east side of the cattle market in Gloucester to unite in a field in Wootton St. Mary and thence through Stonehouse, Stroud, Chalford and Kemble to a junction with the Great Western where it crosses the North Wilts Canal near Swindon, with a branch from Kemble to a piece of land called Botany Bay in Cirencester"—alas, the initial link to Cirencester is now gone.

The Wilts, Somerset and Weymouth Railway

By 1844 railways were being built in many parts of the country, in fact building railways was developing into the Railway Mania; money was available and existing railways were paying good dividends. With G.W.R. assistance a number of companies were formed to extend the broad gauge system, including the Wilts, Somerset and Weymouth Railway to run from Thingley junction, near Chippenham to Melksham, Trowbridge, Westbury (1848), Frome (1850), Dorchester and Weymouth, with branches to Devizes (1857), Bradford-on-Avon (1857), Warminster (1851) and Salisbury (1856). The building of the lines was not continuous due to financial problems, but was spread over a number of years, the dates in brackets show the opening of the various sections. These lines remain in service with the exception of Holt Junction (between Melksham and Bradford) and Devizes.

The Berks and Hants Railway

Apart from giving financial assistance, as to the W. S. & W.R., the G.W.R. promoted some lines by means of subsidiary companies, providing the subscription capital and the Directors. One of these companies was the Berks and Hants whose line ran from Reading to Newbury, Hungerford and Basingstoke and whose Bill was passed in 1845. The line opened to Hungerford in December 1847 and to Basingstoke in November 1848, being delayed because of the difficult negotiations with the L.S.W. for G.W. accommodation alongside the former's station (echo of the bad relations between the two companies!).

The negotiations for a line west from Hungerford to Devizes, i.e. the B. & H. extension, had become involved in the 'battle' between the G.W. and L.S.W., who were both seeking to go west from Salisbury. In 1847 both the G.W. Berks & Hants extension and the L.S.W. supported Salisbury–Yeovil Bills succeeded in Parliament. The B. & H. extension reached Devizes in 1862 and was one of the two short cuts to the West Country, the other being the Patney to Westbury line.

The other G.W. link to shorten the 'route to the West' was made by erecting a station, Patney & Chirton, at the point to which the Hungerford-Devizes line had already been doubled, and then carrying the double line on to Westbury. This 'short cut' line Patney/Westbury shortened the distance to Weymouth, but it was not until Castle Cary and Langport were linked in 1906 that the route to the west was actually made shorter.

Again on this theme—on 1st January 1903 the first section of a more direct route to South Wales, avoiding Bath and Bristol was established by the opening of a Wootton Bassett–Badminton line, which was extended to Patchway (and Filton curve) in July.

Other Branches
Other branch railways in Wiltshire were built to satisfy local demand, the capital and operation being of G.W. origin—the most important were:

(i) *Calne Railway*—Chippenham to Calne, broad gauge, worked by G.W., opened in 1863, absorbed by G.W. 1892.
(ii) *Marlborough Railway*—Savernake to Marlborough, broad gauge, worked by G.W., opened in 1864, absorbed by G.W. 1896.
(iii) *Malmesbury Railway*—Dauntsey to Malmesbury, narrow gauge, worked by G.W., opened in 1877. absorbed by G.W. in 1880.
(iv) *Swindon & Highworth Railway*—Highworth Junction to Highworth, narrow gauge, worked by G.W., opened in 1883.

The London and South Western Railway
This was the other contestant in the battle to build a railway to the West Country across Wiltshire. When its Act was gained in 1834 for a railway between London and Southampton, the Company followed the common practice of naming it by its geographical extremities and hence became the London and Southampton Railway. Construction began under Francis Giles and later Joseph Locke and developed from both ends—first to Woking in May 1838, then to Basingstoke in June 1839. At about this time Winchester had been reached from Southampton and the line was opened throughout on 11th May 1840.

It was with an eye on heading west to Bath and Bristol that the L.S.W. built west from London around 'the great bend of Basingstoke' before turning south towards Winchester and Southampton. By the time a branch had been opened from Bishopstoke (now Eastleigh) to Gosport in 1842 the name of the Company had been changed to the London and South Western Railway, in keeping with the ambition to build westwards.

Although failing to succeed with the 'Basing to Bath Railway' which they supported, the L.S.W. were not immediately discouraged and the line west from Southampton to Dorchester was acquired in 1847—in addition they continued their westward drive by opening a double line from Bishopstoke, via Chandlers Ford and Romsey to Salisbury. This scheme "to terminate near Smith's Close, otherwise Fowler's Croft, at Milford in Salisbury, by the turnpike road to Southampton" was authorised in July 1844 and the line opened to Milford station for "coal and goods" on 27th January 1847 and for passenger traffic on 1st March.

The L.S.W. did not pursue this western route so vigorously but eventually pressure for a more direct line to London and an agreed division of territory with the G.W.R. led to the building of the line from Basingstoke, which reached Andover Junction in 1854 and Salisbury (Milford Station) in 1857.

The Salisbury to Yeovil Railway was sponsored by the L.S.W. as the next step, the Salisbury to Gillingham section being opened by 2nd May 1859 and the line on to Yeovil by 1st June 1860.

The station situation arising at this time in Salisbury is of interest—there was the G.W. terminus on the west side of Fisherton Street, built when their line reached the city in 1856, while the 1847 L.S.W. station at Milford in addition to being away from the centre of the city, was operationally inconvenient as the London trains had to reverse into it. When this terminal station was extensively damaged by fire in 1858 it was decided by the L.S.W. to build on a new site on the east side of Fisherton Street, and opposite the G.W. terminus. The city authorities, however, refused the level crossing which would permit a link with the Salisbury and Yeovil line then being built and therefore had to have the S. & Y. station adjacent to that of the G.W. This new L.S.W. station had to go alongside, or on the same level as the G.W. one. In addition there was a difference in the ground levels between Milford and Fisherton Street such that there was a need for a sharp curve, cuttings, embankments and a short tunnel to the new L.S.W./S. & Y. joint station. It was completed in May 1859 with the station buildings on a long platform on the Down side of the line and Up platform on the east side of Fisherton Street.

The present combined station was built and completed in 1902, while the Milford station remained as a goods yard until recent years. In 1883 a short new line was built from the 'new' L.S.W. station to a goods terminus at one end of the Market Square and the facade of this terminus remains as the front of the new Library building opened in 1975—there are, therefore, some remnants of early railways to be seen in the Salisbury area, at Milford, Fisherton Street and the Market Square.

L.S.W. Branches in Wiltshire

Salisbury and Dorset Junction Railway
The Act of 1861 authorised the linking of the L.S.W. at Alderbury Junction, east of Salisbury on the Basingstoke–Salisbury line, with the Southampton and Dorset Railway at West Moors, but the Act was secured against the goodwill of the L.S.W. (which eventually worked the line, taking 45% of the receipts!) as they had emphasised it was unnecessary.

However, the Salisbury traders and farmers considered that the rail route to Wimbourne, Poole and South Devon via the Southampton line was time-consuming and costly. The work on the new line was begun on 3rd February 1864 when "a cheery crowd saw Countess Nelson from nearby Trafalgar House at Downton, cut the first sod".

The line was opened on 1st January 1866 when, it is recorded, "the bells of the Cathedral at Salisbury pealed joyfully", but without ensuring success, as the L.S.W. continued to use every lawful means to prove their forecasting correct, and finally purchased the line cheaply in 1883. The line was closed in B.R. days.

Swindon, Marlborough and Andover Railway
This southern section of the Midland and South Western Junction Railway received authority on 21st July 1873 to construct lines from the G.W. at Swindon, to the Marlborough Railway at Marlborough and from the G.W., Berks and Hants line at Savernake, to the L.S.W. line at Abbots Ann, about 2.4 km (1½ miles) west of Andover Junction Station. The lines opened to Marlborough on 5th February 1881 and from Savernake to Andover Junction Station on 1st May 1882, using the L.S.W. line from Red Post until the line alongside was ready on 19th November 1882. The M. & S.W. Junction line north of Swindon (Town), the Swindon and Cheltenham extension to Cirencester (Watermoor), was opened in 1883. On this line through from Cirencester to Andover there were alternative stations at Cirencester, Swindon, Savernake and Andover, surely representing the independence of the early railway companies.

Military Railways
At the turn of the century Salisbury Plain began to be developed as a training area for the armed services, as well as a storage area, at the expense of Aldershot, because of the suitability of the ground and the relative proximity of the embarkation port of Southampton. The next step was to provide the railway connections capable of rapidly assembling and dispersing the large numbers of men, horses and military vehicles, as well as quantities of stores and ammunition. These military railways became linked with Andover and the Swindon, Marlborough and Andover Railway lines at Ludgershall and Tidworth and with the L.S.W. at Amesbury and Bulford. There are many features of the line e.g. embankments, cuttings, bridges, etc., still in existence, related to the system known as:

Amesbury and Military Camps Railway
This light railway to Amesbury was constructed under an Order of 1898 and it left the L.S.W. main line about 3.2 km (2 miles) west of Grateley Station and was opened to the public as well as for military traffic on 2nd June 1902. In 1904 the main line link was altered and through running between Amesbury and Salisbury was introduced. The line was extended to Bulford and opened to public use on 1st June 1906, being continued to the Bulford camps at the same time. The Ludgershall to Tidworth branch, which was built by the War Office and leased to the S.M. & A.R. under an agreement on 19th November, 1900, was opened for public use on 1st October, 1902.

On the outbreak of war in 1914, development of the military railways in the area accelerated, as the three small hangers of the Bristol Aeroplane Company, then very early in the business of flying were soon, with other aerodromes and camps, e.g. Larkhill, Boscombe Down and so on, linked by light railways. After 1919 their use fell away although in 1939–45 Amesbury again had a brief revival as a centre for troop movements—there were regular public trains between Bulford and Salisbury until after nationalisation in 1947. Little of substance remains to be seen but there are numerous reminders on the routes of the lines.

Abortive Lines
This subject could provide years of study, the number of projected railways which did not materialise is legion and mention can be made of only a few.

(a) Amesbury and Military Camps railway of 1898. The original plans envisaged the line going on from Larkhill to Shrewton, but this was not laid. In 1917 there were proposals to extend the Bulford line through to Tidworth, but these were not implemented because the route would have interfered with the rifle ranges.

(b) In *Bradshaw's Railway Manual* (*Shareholder's Guide & Directory 1869*) there were proposals in 1865 to construct a line from the L.S.W. at Idmiston (Wilts) to Pewsey on the G.W. Berks and Hants line—length 28 km (17½ miles) which never materialised.

(c) The Avon Valley Route. In the 1974 issue of the *Salisbury and South Wilts Industrial Archeology Society Journal*, D. W. J. Thody described in detail the abortive efforts made to establish a north-south line through the Avon Valley from Pewsey to Salisbury during the years 1866–98, when the presence of the Army on Salisbury Plain became the dominant influence; the route across the valley from the L.S.W. Waterloo line being built instead, as set out above. Mr. Thody speculates on the environmental questions which would arise today should a north-south route be in question.

THE RAILWAYS OF WILTSHIRE

Great Western and Associated Railways

Date of opening	*Railway*	*Section Constructed*
1840	G.W.	Line reached Faringdon Road (now Challow)
1840	G.W.	Bristol to Bath
1840	G.W.	Faringdon Road to Hay Lane
1841	G.W.	Hay Lane to Chippenham
1841	C. & G.W.U.	Swindon to Cirencester (Town)
1841	G.W.	Chippenham to Bath—line through Paddington/Bristol
1847	G.W.	Reading to Hungerford
1848	G.W.	Reading to Basingstoke
1848	W, S. & W.	Thingley to Westbury via Melksham & Trowbridge
1850	W, S. & W.	Westbury to Frome
1851	W, S. & W.	Westbury to Warminster
1856	W, S. & W.	Warminster to Salisbury
1857	W, S. & W.	Holt Junction to Devizes
1862	G.W.	Hungerford to Devizes via Pewsey
1863	C.R.	Chippenham to Calne (G.W. operated)
1864	Mh.R.	Savernake to Marlborough (High level)
1877	My.R.	Dauntsey to Malmesbury (G.W. operated)
1883	S. & H.R.	Highworth Junction to Highworth (G.W. operated)
1900	G.W.	Patney to Westbury
1903	G.W.	Badminton to Patchway and link with South Wales

London and South Western Railway and Associated Railways

1839	L. & S.	Line reached Southampton via Basingstoke
1842	L. & S.	Branch to Gosport (name of railway changed to L.S.W.)
1847	L.S.W.	Bishopstoke (Eastleigh) to Salisbury (Milford)
1857	L.S.W.	Basingstoke to Salisbury (Milford)
1859	S. & Y.	Salisbury to Gillingham (L.S.W. operated)
1860	S. & Y.	Line reached Yeovil
1866	S. & D. Jct.	Salisbury to West Moors
1881	S.M. & A.	Swindon (Town) to Marlborough (Low Level)
1882	S.M. & A.	Savernake to Andover
1883	M. & S.W. Jct.	Swindon (Town) to Cirencester (Watermoor)
1898	M. & G.	Savernake to Marlborough (Low Level)

Railway Names

G.W.	Great Western Railway
C. & G.W.U.	Cheltenham and Great Western Union Railway
W, S. & W.	Wilts, Somerset and Weymouth Railway
C.R.	Calne Railway
Mh.R.	Marlborough Railway
My.R.	Malmesbury Railway
S. & H.R.	Swindon and Highworth Railway
L. & S.	London and Southampton Railway
L.S.W.	London and South Western Railway
S. & Y.	Salisbury and Yeovil Railway
S. & D. Jct.	Salisbury and Dorset Junction Railway
S.M. & A.	Swindon, Marlborough and Andover Railway
M. & S.W. Jct.	Midland and South Western Junction Railway
M. & G.	Marlborough and Grafton Railway

Swindon: The front of Swindon Station at the turn of the century. Note the G.W.R. motor bus and horse carriage (Photo., British Rail)

Box: The west portal of Box Tunnel. Showing broad gauge track of bridge rails on longitudinal timbers. (Photo., British Rail)

Great Wishford: The goods shed at Wishford Station, formerly an important collection point for agricultural produce from a wide area

Gazetteer

Tramroads (Sites Only)

1. Conkwell
2. Murhill
3. Caen Hill, Devizes

Great Western Railway

4. Swindon Railway Station
5. Swindon Workshops
6. Great Western Railway Museum
7. Chippenham Railway Station
8. Chippenham Viaduct
9. Great Somerford Viaduct
10. Box Tunnel
11. Middle Hill Tunnel
12. Pewsey Railway Station
13. Bradford-on-Avon Station
14. Trowbridge Station
15. Bradford-on-Avon Tunnel

London and South Western Railway

16. Market Hall Railway Station (now Salisbury Library)
17. Salisbury Railway Station

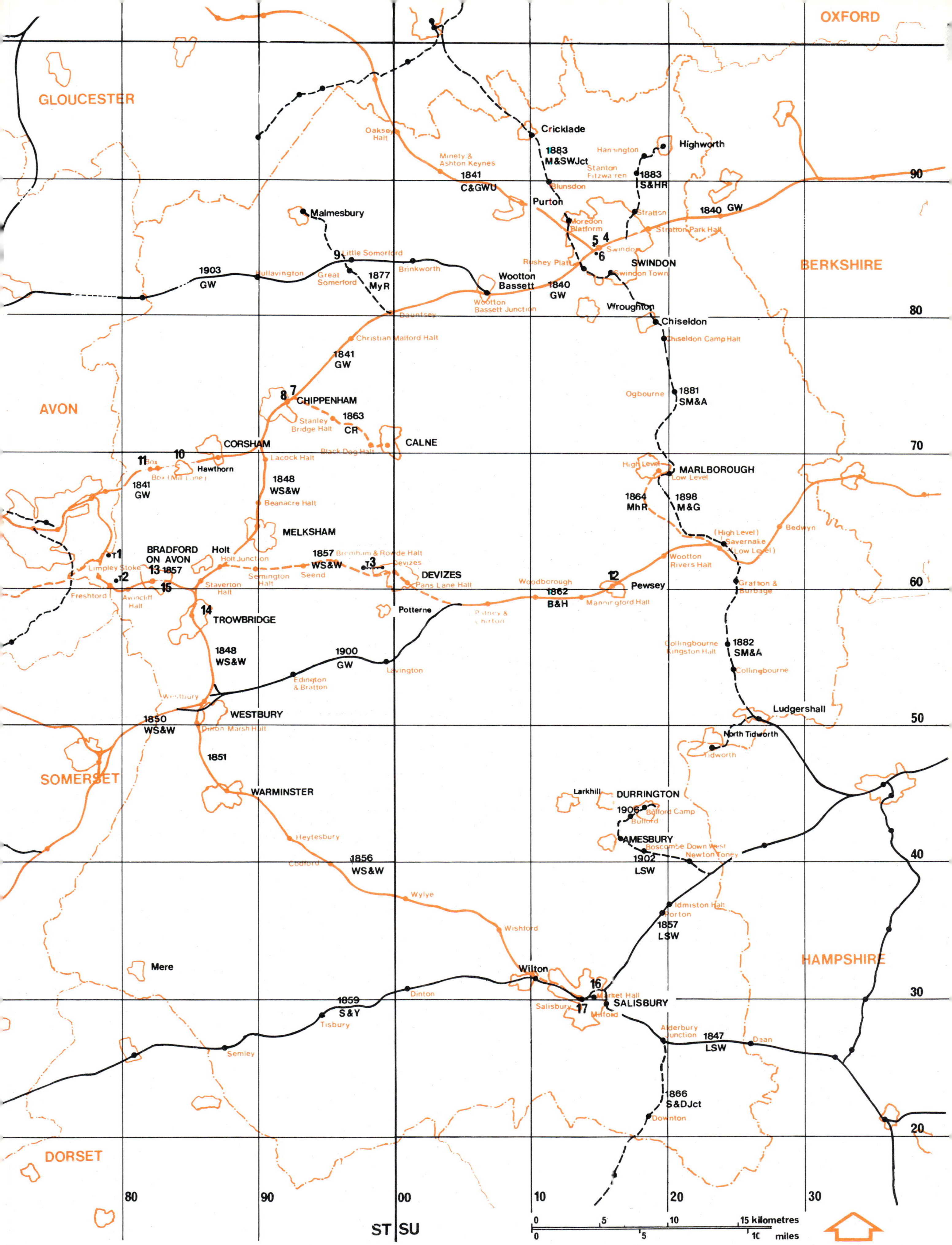

RAILWAYS, showing dates of original construction

first constructed in broad gauge — standard gauge — now closed — •T3 tramroad — 1898/M&G line constructed / original company

2. POWER

2a. Animal Power

The use of animal energy to turn machinery by direct action and later, by gear turning, was developed from the later Middle Ages together with water- and wind-power. At Vasterne, in Wootton Bassett, a horse-mill worth 10s. per annum is recorded on the manor in 1281, also two water mills and one windmill, an indication of the need for rotary power to drive mills in all conditions. Horse mills for corn and malt milling are referred to in a manorial context into the 16th century and after, but no details of their form or remains are known. In the 18th century horse-power was used to drive mills, but this was generally in association with an industry, such as brewing, and the horses turned large diameter horizontal gears from which spur drives were taken to millstones and pumps as required.

The use of the treadwheel to raise and lower heavy loads was known in classical antiquity and what is perhaps a 13th century treadwheel, turned by man-power and used to raise building materials, remains at the base of the spire of Salisbury Cathedral (SU 143 295). The wheel is of timber construction with a ladder-like rim. Similar treadwheels turned by donkeys were used to raise water from deep wells, particularly on the edge of the chalk downs. A fine example remains *in situ* at Lower Upham Farm, Chiseldon (SU 208 777), where the timber wheel is 4.26 m (14 ft) in diameter by 1.1176 m (3 ft 8 in) wide. The square shaft on which the wheel turns is rounded for part of its length to form a winding drum for the rope. This wheel is possibly of late 17th century origin, and the well which it once served is now sealed. A second example has been re-erected in the museum at Lackham College of Agriculture, Lacock, and came from New Farm, Stratford Toney (SU 093 237). This wheel is 3.96 m (13 ft) diameter by 1.22 m (4 ft) wide and probably of later date than the Lower Upham Farm wheel.

Also in the museum at Lackham College is an excellent collection of 'drowner's' tools together with an Archimedean screw which was used for lifting water from the river into the carriages. The screw was made at Britford, Salisbury, in 1830 and is a good example of a village wheelwright's work consisting of a wooden cylinder bound with iron hoops with the screw formed of sheet metal nailed to a central timber axis. At one end of the axis is a universal joint to which was attached an iron shaft rotated by a horse-gear, in this case, a portable iron gear consisting of an inverted iron bevel gear which was turned by the horse and drove a pinion on the end of the tumble-bar, thus rotating the screw.

In the 19th century several textile factories in the county were driven by horses, three or four horses being commonly used to turn overhead gears from which drives were taken to machines on each floor of the building. While documentary evidence can be found, no actual examples are known to have survived.

Wooden overhead gears were also used on farms to drive threshing machines and later, other barn machinery. The roundhouses which protected these gears and the horses that worked them from the weather, can be seen as extensions to barns on several Wiltshire farms. A good example survives, without the gears, at Horningsham (ST 820 415). The lack of a great number of roundhouses, compared with north-east England and Scotland, is probably due to the later adoption of the threshing machine in the south and west. By the time threshers were well established in Wiltshire—after the machine breaking riots of 1830–2 when some 97 were smashed in the county—portable iron gears were available. These were supplied by, and often manufactured by, local ironworks and agricultural engineers, such as Reeves of Bratton who advertised their own horse- and pony-gears well into the 20th century. These gears could be set up in the open farm yard and used to drive any number of farm machines, intermediate gearing motions being supplied to enable the speed ratio to be increased. Edwin Ratcliffe of Westport Iron Works, Malmesbury, also supplied and maintained horse-gears.

Another agricultural use of horse-power is illustrated by the cider mills, in which a vertical stone roller on a shaft pulled by a horse ran in a chase cut into the horizontal stone base and apples put into the chase were crushed to pulp. Several examples survive in various stages of decay, a good example standing outside the Red Lion Inn, Avebury (SU 102 699) with a cider press close by.

An interesting example of a small animal treadwheel exists in the bar of the George Inn, Lacock (ST 915 684), built into the return wall of a fireplace. This wheel, 0.89 m (2 ft 11 in) diameter by 0.22 m (8¾ in) wide, was turned by a dog to turn a roasting spit before the fire. The dogs which turned these wheels were a specific breed, appropriately known as 'Turnspits'.

2b. Wind-power

Although the use of water-power is widely accepted in the county, many windmills also existed, particularly on the edges of the chalk downs and in exposed locations where watermills were not viable but human settlement demanded a source of milled grain.

The earliest reference yet known to a windmill in Wiltshire is from Ebbesbourne Wake, a windmill on the manor of 'Hebelsburnel' being worth one mark per annum in 1248. A windmill is recorded at Winterbourne Monkton *c.* 1265 and from the 1270s onwards references occur more frequently. The medieval windmills were an important part of manorial economy; on the manor of Sherston, for example, a windmill valued 2s., a horse mill worth 10s and 3 watermills worth 36s. are recorded in 1375 and the density of these corn-mills is perhaps explained in part by a reference of 1349 to two watermills on the same manor being worth 20s. a year "and not more because they cannot grind in summertime".

Little is known of the form of these early windmills, but they are likely to have been timber post mills; windmills of this type survived until the end of the 19th century, particularly on Salisbury Plain where there was a lack of good building stone. The materials used for windmill building tend to follow the same pattern as the local buildings. County maps of the late 18th and early 19th centuries show many windmills all round the county and the heyday of mill construction was in the early 19th century, perhaps the result of increased pressure on the county's corn milling activity due to the Napoleonic Wars.

Although over 90 specific sites and references have been located, surviving evidence is sparse, many sites proving to be empty when visited. Probably the last evidence of a Wiltshire post mill can be seen in the chancel roof of the Church of St. Thomas à Beckett in Tilshead, which was partly rebuilt early this century using timbers from the dismantled post mill which once stood above the village. Illustrations show this post mill to have a thatched roof and vertically boarded roundhouse and to have worked with two common and two shuttered sails—a good working combination of power and self-regulation. At Collingbourne Kingston a mound, which now contains a reservoir, marks the site of a windmill shown on Andrews' and Drury's map of 1773 and subsequently rebuilt sometime after 1820. In 1840 the mill was referred to as being "covered with boards" and contained "three pairs of millstones, wire machines and dressing mills". This mill appears to have worked until the 1870s.

The masonry shell of the tower mill has made it more capable of survival in some form and the remains of several towers can be seen; Wilton Windmill, Grafton, has recently been well restored and is a good example of a 19th century Wiltshire tower mill. At Aldbourne a brick tower mill which had a dome-shaped cap, four shuttered sails and a fantail—similar in appearance to Wilton Mill—was pulled down in 1900, the last of several windmills in the parish, where references date back to the early 14th century.

The form of the Wiltshire tower mills varies from east to west of the county, those to the east being of brick with the improvements of the 18th and 19th centuries—the shuttered sails and fantail, for example—having been adopted, while those on the west side are more reminiscent of their Somerset neighbours. All too little is known at present, however, of the form of many of the mills to make confident assumptions, and those rebuilt or built from the 1820s would most likely have taken advantage of the improved technology and the availability of iron mill-work.

Tower Mill Remains:

Bradford-on-Avon (ST 828 612)
An almost parallel-sided ashlar stone tower, now with a low-pitched conical roof and overhanging eaves, can be seen to the north of the town centre. It was working in 1809 when a new windmiller was advertised for, but by 1864 it was referred to as 'Old Mill' and evidently converted to a dwelling.

Brinkworth (SU 031 853)
There is evidence of some five windmills in Brinkworth from the later middle ages, the last being a windmill referred to as "new-built" in 1832. This was the stone tower mill, unusual in that the tower was hung with split-stone tiles and the mill had six sails; part of the base and remains of the outbuildings can be seen. In the early 1870s it was converted to work by steam power, the new mill-work being installed by Edwin Ratcliffe of the Westport Iron Works, Malmesbury, and in 1929 it was powered by a gas engine. The masonry tower has been reduced to almost foundation level over the last few years.

Chiseldon (SU 190 799)
The complete brick shell of this tower survives, apparently a 19th century mill which went out of commission by the late 1890s. All the openings have been blocked and there is evidence of a stage at first floor level.

Devizes (SU 001 614)
At Devizes two brick tower mills were built on the castle mound in the early 18th century. They are shown on a drawing by William Stukeley of 1723 and a fine trade card of William Leach "Snuff-maker at the Windmills in Devizes" clearly depicts them. It is said that they were built for crushing oil seed, converted for snuff milling in the 1750s and later used for grinding corn. Part of the northern tower still stands, much altered, to become part of the castle in about 1840.

West Gomeldon, Idmiston (SU 177 358)
A fine, tapering flint and brick tower, rendered externally, although gutted internally, stands at the edge of a wood. The iron windshaft and iron arms of the brake-wheel, as well as part of the fantail gearing, survive high up on the decayed cap framing. The mill is said to have been built about 1840 and ceased work about 1885.

East Knoyle (ST 874 310)
This steeply battered stone tower is raised on a circular masonry and earth platform and survives as a summer-house. It was built as a windmill in the late 18th or early 19th century on a site traditionally known as Windmill Hill. Old pictures show the mill with a gable cap and tailbox containing the winding gear—in the Somerset manner—and two common sails. The mill ceased work late in the 19th century, was burnt out about 1912 and subsequently converted.

Wilton Windmill, Grafton (SU 276 617)
Wilton Windmill was built in 1821 by or for J. Gale on a site which was not previously occupied by a windmill. It is a brick tower mill, with a dome-shaped cap and two common (cloth set) and two patent shuttered sails which are turned into the wind by a six-bladed fantail. The mill-work represents much of the skill of the 19th century millwright, with cast iron shafting and gearing which drives two pairs of 1.22 m (4 ft) diameter stones. There were originally three pairs of millstones. When built the tower was surrounded by low outbuildings which must have provided a working platform for the miller to adjust the sails from, but now there is a timber stage around the tower. The mill has been restored as a fine, workable example of an industrial monument in Wiltshire.

2c. Annular Vaned Windpumps

The lattice tower with a multiblade windwheel has since the end of the last century become a common, if not often noticed, feature of the British landscape. Although this method of obtaining windpower has been put to many uses including the grinding of grain and the generation of electricity, its most common and continuing usage is water pumping.

In this field its applications have been widespread, estates, their mansions, dwellings and farmsteads, early local authority and local initiative water supply schemes —such as that at Upton Scudamore in 1906—as well as larger dwellings. A windpump, removed it is thought *c.* 1938 at 'Ashmore House', Whiteparish was one example of this type of use. Its most frequent employment, however, must be found in farmsteads and in the watering of outlying fields. Here the automatic control by means of the tail vane and brake and the robust galvanised construction were obvious boons.

In Wiltshire a number, albeit declining, of annular vaned windpumps survive in various states of repair or disrepair. Few of these are capable of work or could easily be made so and even fewer are actually in continuous operation. There is a number of reasons for this decline, primarily, perhaps, the advent of a reasonable mains electricity supply and the efficient submersible pump. With the discontinued usage and removal of many, an historic vicious circle was set up whereby the facilities for the maintenance of the survivors became less available and more costly, and lacking attention they suffered wind damage and in turn fell into ruin and were superseded. The effects of lowered water tables resulting from deep pumping have doubtless made others less useful sources, if not put them out of operation altogether. With changing economic conditions and the rising capital costs of laying pipelines, or taking electricity supplies a long distance, as well as increased running costs, the case for the windpump, despite the effects of water nationalisation, may be improving.

Their use throughout the county has been extensive both on the downs and in the valleys. Examples of the work of many manufacturers and erectors remain, covering a period from the latter part of the 19th century until almost the present day. Among these are John Wallis Titt of the Woodcock Ironworks, Warminster, one of the pioneers of this type of equipment with their canvas bladed 'Simplex' and 'Woodcock' and later 'Imperial' metal vaned types. Their association with the town date from the 1860s. Hole and Roberts of the same place was another, but shortlived, Wiltshire maker.

Some of the county's earlier windpumps represent the work of Duke and Ockenden of Littlehampton, water engineers, whose continuing history extends, like Titt's and E. H. Roberts' of Deanshanger in Northamptonshire, from the second half of the last century. The latter company failed in the twenties and its 'Hercules' trade name was acquired by H. J. Godwin of Quenington, Gloucestershire, who supplied many of the more recent examples of windpump. Represented as well is Thomas and Son of Worcester, a firm which no longer exists but whose 'Climax' oil bath type is probably the most widespread type of windpump in the country and widely exported.

These later pumps would have been erected and serviced by the manufacturers themselves or local engineers such as Wallis Titt or John Mullins & Son of Colerne and Bath in Somerset. Often an earlier tower was modernised by the replacement of the original open gearing or crank with an enclosed oil bath while a windwheel might be replaced several times in the life of a tower. Standby power, or arrangements for providing it, in the form of a small internal combustion engine might also be added. Often the pumps would be sited near the reservoir, although in some cases a main of perhaps a mile in length might be provided to a suitably elevated position, to the house or to the cattle troughs to be served.

Some Annular Vaned Windpumps in Wiltshire

Broad Hinton–Uffcot (SU 122 768)
Visible on the 600 ft contour to the east of the A361 Avebury to Wroughton road, an early tower by E. & H. Roberts updated by the fitting of an oil bath and 18 blade wheel by T. H. White of Devizes.

Crudwell–Chelworth Cross Roads (ST 966 951)
A large 24 bladed unit made and erected in 1930 by H. J. Godwin. Complete but now disused and suffering from wind damage.

Steeple Ashton–Spiers Piece (ST 916 557)
In this arrangement by John Mullins & Son the head and wheel are placed above the tank they serve—a method well suited to locations without suitable elevations. Only the radial spokes of the wheel remain although tail vane and oil bath are complete and *in situ.*

Wilsford (SU 092 562)
In the Vale of Pewsey a landmark well known to users of the A342 Devizes to Upavon road. A 'Climax' unit with a disproportionately large wheel on a dumpy tower with reservoir adjacent and to the south.

Winterslow–Lopcombe Corner (SU 251 354 and SU 253 354)
The two windpumps on this road junction have long been familiar to those entering the county on the A30 Stockbridge to Salisbury road. The former is now merely a tower while the latter is the top stage, head, platform and wheel of a pump moved a short distance from its original position. This, with the wheel gaily painted, now serves as an advertising feature!

Wylye (SU 008 373)
Visible in a farm yard to the south of the railway station it was built to serve. Although 24 blades have been removed this windpump is otherwise complete and of great interest not only as an early example but as one of the very few open gear units surviving erected by Titt.

Wylye–Deptford (SU 015 384)
On the other side of the Wylye Valley and in the north-east angle of the junction formed by the A303 and the A36 Warminster to Wilton road and seen to best advantage from the latter road east of the junction complex. A later oil bath type in substantially complete and good order.

2d. Water-power

A large part of Wiltshire has always enjoyed an ample supply of water, even in periods of drought the main river systems have good flows. Their rate of fall has contributed to their early and widespread use for driving watermills. By Saxon times there were few settlements in Wiltshire which were without a watermill, or at least a share in one. Our earliest record, the *Domesday Survey*, shows that the county had over 300 mills besides a number of shares, some of which may have fallen beyond the present county boundary. In fact at that date, 1086, the county ranked third in all England, while the settlements of the Wylye Valley had a greater density of mills than any other area in the country.

At least a hundred of the Domesday mill sites can be traced on the ground, and although all existing mill structures are rebuildings, the channels, weirs and hatches are probably on the old sites which had been found suitable. The contour leats, such as that at Crookwood Mill Farm (SU 023 585) winding for over 0.8 km ($\frac{1}{2}$ mile) must represent jealously guarded water rights of long standing.

At the time of Domesday all mills were used for grinding corn, although soon after the potential of the power thus generated was recognised as having other uses.

The first of these applications, and one which was to have a dramatic effect upon the economy of the county, was to convert the rotary motion of the mill to a reciprocating motion which was used in the fulling of cloth. One of the earliest references to a fulling mill in England was in 1189 in a charter of Richard I confirming the holdings of Stanley Abbey, near Calne; detailed accounts also exist for the building of a mill at Marlborough in 1237. The carpenters included in their accounts the making and adjusting of *flagella et baterella*, the hammers of the mill. At Wilton Felt Factory the fulling stocks were powered by water until well into the present century.

Gig mills made their appearance in the 15th century. In these mills cloths which were to have their naps raised were passed over water-driven rollers set with teazles. Previously this task had been done by hand. In the 16th century the power of the mill was used in the manufacture of paper, the basic requirements for which were a sufficient head to drive the machinery and a good supply of clear water. One of the earliest of these mills was at Bemerton in West Harnham parish which was probably founded in the mid-sixteenth century.

The 19th century saw the water and windmills employed in the grinding of snuff, mills at Calstone, Whistley and Poulshot being used for this purpose, while in Devizes wind and donkey power were similarly employed.

The ultimate use of water power was in the generation of electricity. The Downton Electric Light Company operated from a mill on the Avon, and the Town Mill in Salisbury was similarly used. Latterly many corn mills have been converted to residences but the wheels and turbines retained to generate domestic power.

The use to which many mills were put changed many times in the course of their history, and it would be wrong to assume that the preponderance of grain mills surviving was always so used.

The Industrial Revolution's main effects are best studied by reference to the increasing use of cast iron in the machinery and the application of mechanical power to the movement of materials within the mills. Whilst the actual water-wheel took readily to the use of the new materials, the types of wheel illustrate the design changes wrought by their adoption. The earliest use shows as cast iron naves, fitted to wooden shafts and clasping wooden arms. The cast iron rim, still with wooden floats, but usually with iron starts and retaining the flexibility of wooden spokes is a logical development. The late 19th century all-metal wheel mounted on cast iron shafts, but fitted with wrought iron ventilated buckets, is the high tide of water-wheel development, only to be superseded early in this century when the reaction turbine's reliability proved its value as a replacement in so many of our mills.

In the water driven mills the introduction of iron gearing became general with mixed materials to give a smooth drive. Usually the second gear—the driven one—would be iron but wooden teeth in an iron frame would be retained as the primary drive. This allowed the sweet running associated with wooden gears, with the assurance that if a jam occurred only a wooden cog would need replacement. The form of gear tooth used was still a derivative of the wooden form.

Other applications stemming from the inventive era are to be found in the mechanism applied for tentering the mill; i.e. the fine adjustment of the running stone to control the fineness of the flour. A noteworthy feature which perhaps originated nearby in Ringwood, Hants. is the massive cast footstep bearing used to bridge the main shelf and support the vertical shaft, this is sometimes known as the Armfield Arch.

However, although some cast iron wheel shafts exist, as at South Newton, (SU 088 339) the majority of corn mills retained their traditional wooden shafts until the 20th century, when the introduction of the reaction turbine rendered them obsolete.

The early 19th century had seen the French Burr grindstone become the standard for grinding wheat, but Derbyshire Millstone Grit, Quartz Conglomerate, and Patent Composition stones are all recorded. The stones seldom travel far once they are discarded, and many remain visible or are even used as display features. There are a pair of French Burrs and another of Peaks set on edge in a hedge alongside the A354 near Coombe Bissett at (SU 106 261). A single lower stone of Quartz

Conglomerate has been set in the wall of a small outbuilding behind Harnham Mill (SU 134 295). Another single stone is set in the wall of the steps leading to Littlecot Mill at Enford, now a private dwelling (SU 142 518). At Mere in the south-west, just off the A30, a single French Burr has been set in the embankment of the stream (ST 815 324).

SELECTED WATERMILLS

Bristol Avon

Avoncliff Mills (ST 805 601)
The weir on this site is probably ancient, and was built to give a steady supply of water to the two mills at either end of the weir. Daniel Mill on the south side of the river is a former textile mill; equipped with machinery in 1791, this is the first reference to water powered machinery in Wiltshire in the cloth manufacturing trade. The machinery, housed in an undercroft, is a vertical turbine generating electricity and driving a wood saw. Old Mill, on the north side, was a fulling mill, converted to corn milling in 1860 with a breast-wheel by J. Barrett of Twerton, Bath, under an iron cantilevered extension.

River Marden

Hazeland Mill (ST 972 723)
A fulling mill since the 16th century and extended in the 19th century. The decline of the cloth industry led to its conversion to corn milling in the 1830s. The turbine is still in good order, last used in 1970.

Blacklands Mill, Calne (SU 017 694)
A two storey red brick cornmill with a breastshot wheel housed in an attached wheelhouse. The mill-house and pond have been restored.

By Brook

Drewett's Mill, Box (ST 833 698)
Formerly an overshot wheel 3.04 m (10 ft) diameter, 1.52 m (5 ft) wide which drove three pairs of stones. Now a vertical reaction turbine driving only two pairs of stones and a saw bench. Still in use.

Semington Brook

Baldham Mill, Seend (ST 927 598)
This mill was held by Mary Baldenham in 1371 as a fulling mill; until 1976 operated by J. & J. Noad and Co. who also owned the two mills below Baldham. The mill was turbine driven, the turbine is to be used to generate electricity and formerly drove a pair of horizontal stones, dressing machines and steaming plant.

Seend Head Mill (ST 922 599)
The second of Noad's mills comprises the mill and mill-house with ancillary mill buildings.

Littleton Mill (ST 912 606)
Also owned until 1976 by the Noads, the site of the 1803 machine breaking riot which led to the execution of Thomas Hilliker, a shearman of Trowbridge. The mill was fitted out as a cornmill by G. Dunford and Son of Great Cheverell about 1887. The water-wheel was replaced by a turbine in 1926, and the four pairs of Peak stones were replaced by two pairs of vertical stones by Barron of Gloucester. Barley was milled commercially until 1976.

Summerham Brook

Rowde Mill (ST 973 628)
A large overshot wheel by Armfields of Ringwood 4.27 m (14 ft) diameter by 1.37 m (4 ft 5 in) wide driving two pairs of stones. Ceased operation in late 1940s. The millwright was Dunford of Great Cheverell. An embankment dam nearby at SU 004 633 was intended for a further mill, now a house conversion.

River Kennet

Elcott Mill, Marlborough (SU 204 691)
Now demolished, site only survives.

Durnford Mill, Mildenhall (SU 211 695)
A three storey L-shaped brick mill with a 3.04 m (10 ft) diameter by 1.86 m (6 ft) wide undershot wheel which formerly drove three pairs of stones.

Marden Mill (SU 087 582)
A complex comprising a self-contained brewery, mill, mill-house and public house, A 16 h.p. Armfield Turbine drives a crushing mill, and demonstrations can be arranged with the owner. The mill has a datestone "CB 1842".

Hampshire Avon

Coombe Mill, Enford (SU 148 505)
All the gear except a fine, all-metal external wheel removed during house conversion. The wheel 3.50 m (11 ft 6 in) diameter by 1.52 m (5 ft) wide is visible beyond the house from the road.

Downton (SU 180 215)
Downton tannery still retains its wheel, a 3.04 m (10 ft) diameter by 0.76 m (2 ft 6 in) wide all-metal wheel used to agitate the tan pits. The wheel is clearly visible from the B3080. Due to an unusual arrangement the wheel appears to rotate the wrong way. There are two further mills opposite, both with long histories including papermaking and flour milling.

Town Mill, Salisbury (SU 143 300)
This corn mill on a site traditionally as old as the cathedral has a date stone over a rear window of 1756. Close by is the site of an early fulling mill visible from the footpath to the car park. The city's first generating station alongside originally had a water driven turbine, the intake of which remains. A fine elevation faces Fisherton Bridge.

River Wylye

Harnham Mill, Salisbury (SU 136 295)
The mill itself is now converted to a craft shop and café with the mill race shown as a feature. A single mill stone built into the wall of the small kiln house at the rear reminds one of a recent use as a pottery workshop.

South Newton Mill (SU 088 339)
Working until 1961, a fine all-metal example of an internal breastshot wheel 3.66 m (12 ft) wide driving three pairs of stones. The water supply has been diverted, and the mill-house dated 1711 demolished.

Bishopstrow Mill (ST 897 439)
An electric powered roller mill in a fine building, the water-wheel was still workable until as recently as about 1970. In late 1975 the mill was converted to residential use.

River Nadder

Sutton Mandeville (ST 982 293)
The machinery is still intact, and occasionally used. The condition of the mill building is fair but is in danger of being damaged by the collapse of the adjoining mill cottage. There were two pairs of stones grinding corn.

Tisbury Mill (SU 953 296)
An old stone corn mill used from 1922 by the Tisbury Electricity Supply Co. as a generating station. Now converted to domestic use, the owners generate their own power.

River Bourne

Manor Farm Mill, Winterbourne Gunner (SU 179 355)
A good mill building with adjoining miller's house. A fine Armfield Water Turbine installed in 1924 drives two sets of stones and a crushing mill by Armstrongs of Salisbury. It formerly included a D.C. generator, the only battery charging unit in the area for early radios. The fine modern installation is still in private use.

River Stour

Stourhead Gardens (ST 772 338)
There are two pumping wheels here. The upper is housed in a stone building at right angles to the lower, just to the north of the path. The lower wheel is now working. It is 4.87 m (16 ft) by 0.66 m (2 ft 2 in) wide, overshot, fed by siphon pipe. It is all iron and built by E. S. Hindley & Sons of the Bourton Foundry—just down the road. It is dated 1921. (The upper wheel is similar in all respects, but only 3.65 m (12 ft) diameter and not apparently marked with the maker's name). The wheels both pumped water to a reservoir near Alfred's Tower until *c.* 1970. The pump of the lower (working) wheel is by Godwin of Quenington.

River Ray

Fox Mill, Purton (SU 105 872)
A small mill built behind a fine Georgian-style house, the overshot wheel drove two pairs of stones.

2e. Steam, Gas and Electricity

Steam power came to Wiltshire late in the Industrial Revolution; the principal reason for this would appear to be the difficulties in transporting the fuel required from the nearest coalfields in Somerset. Boulton & Watt of Birmingham record many requests for information in the late 18th century, none of which led to an order. It is not until 1805, the same year that Trowbridge was linked by the Kennet and Avon Canal and the Somerset Coal Canal, that the first engine was installed in the cloth factory of John Cooper in Duke Street; this was only the second to be installed in the South West. An engine does appear to have been ordered in 1802 for the Kennet & Avon Canal, however, it was not installed until 1809.

Several engines were installed between 1805 and the arrival of George Haden in 1815 to install J. &. T. Clark's engine (see page 59). Most engines were Boulton & Watt's but others are known. Charles Taylor's mill at Chippenham used either a Trevithick or a Wolff; a mill at Salisbury advertised an engine by Wood of Oxford for sale in 1812 and another advertisement in 1822 was for the sale of a Bramah engine in a mill at Warminster. Charles Taylor later requested Boulton & Watt to convert his engine to their system.

By 1838 there were some 39 steam-powered mills, which together generated 66% of the total available power; the largest engine was at Angel Mill in Westbury which developed 60 h.p.; it survived until 1939.

Of the engines from this early period the sole surviving examples are those which were installed at Crofton on the Kennet and Avon Canal to raise water 12 m (40 ft) from the reservoir of Wilton Water to the summit. Work started on the engine house in 1800, and the first engine, a Boulton & Watt came into operation in 1809; a second was ordered in 1812. These were low pressure engines, steam for which was generated by three wagon top boilers. The 1812 engine, and possibly the 1809 beam remain from this period.

In 1844 Harveys of Hayle in Cornwall converted the engines to the Cornish Cycle; this conversion raised the operating pressure from the original 4 p.s.i. to 20 p.s.i. and at the same time the wagon top boilers were replaced with Cornish boilers and the 1809 engine was replaced by a Sims Combined engine. In 1905 the three Cornish boilers were replaced by two Lancashire boilers made at the G.W.R. Swindon Works, and the Sims engine, which had not been a success, was rebuilt as a simple condensing engine.

In 1958 the top of the chimney was removed for safety reasons; this reduced the draught through the fire boxes to such an extent that the boilers would not fire effectively. The steam pumps which had been in continuous operation since 1812 were replaced by electric pumps.

The Crofton Society, a branch of the Kennet and Avon Canal Trust, was formed in 1968 with the aim of restoring the engines to use. This work is now complete, and at the time of the restoration the 1812 engine was the oldest working steam engine in the world; it was also the only Boulton & Watt engine doing the work for which it was originally built.

It would be wrong to assume that on the advent of steam power all other power sources were superseded, water-driven factories continued to be developed in those places where a reliable head of water was to be had. Even George Haden, the principal steam engineer in the county, designed water-powered mills, and both Job Wastfield, the Bradford engineer, and the Hadens were recommending the use of poncelet type wheels. In places such as Trowbridge where the stream was unsuited to driving machinery, the steam engine soon replaced other power sources.

Boulton & Watt was also responsible for the development of coal gas-producing plant at the beginning of the 19th century, when the Soho Foundry was the first commercial works to be lit by gas, which was derived from a gas-producing plant installed by William Murdock, the manager. Gas illumination was rapidly installed in many textile mills as it provided a better and safer means of lighting, and enabled the mill owners to operate through the night. It was not until late in the century that gas as a source of power was considered following improvements to Etienne Lenoir's gas engine by N. A. Otto, and the acquisition of a licence to manufacture these engines by F. H. Crossley in 1876. Two mills in Trowbridge were powered by gas engines, Innox and Ashton, the strokes of the engine at the latter could be heard over a large part of the town.

The present century has seen a change from a single power unit driving the whole factory to the use of individual electric motors applied to each machine. Such a system did away with the large losses of power caused by long transmission lines and idling belts. The development of the electric motor came long after the use of electricity for lighting, much the same pattern as had occurred with gas; although there had been electric motors in use since 1879 it was not until improved high pressure alternating current generation and transmission systems were developed that their use became widespread.

Power generation in Wiltshire was initially based on water-powered turbines. The Salisbury Electric Light and Supply Company was founded in 1899 at the Town Mill in the centre of the City where the sluices and hatches for the turbines can still be seen. At Downton the Downton Electric Light Company occupied the mill formerly used by the Jellymans to manufacture paper, the turbine powered generator from this company being used until the mid-1970s when it was acquired for preservation. At the same time the standby diesel generator was also acquired.

The latter half of the present century has seen the closure of the local gas works as the supply has been replaced by North Sea Gas. Only the gas holders survive as a reminder of these undertakings. Similarly the small electric generating stations have been closed as power generation has been concentrated in larger units. One must wonder at the economy of closing a station deriving power from a more or less constant flow of water—even in the unprecedented drought of 1976 the turbines at Baldham & Littleton Mills on the small Seend Brook had a sufficient head of water to run without recourse to standby power sources.

Gazetteer

Animal Power

1. Salisbury Cathedral, treadwheel
2. Lower Upham Farm, Chiseldon, donkeywheel
3. Lackham College Museum, donkeywheel
4. Lackham College Museum, downer's tools and Archimedean Screw
5. Horningsham, barn roundhouse
6. Avebury, cider mill
7. Lacock, dog spit

Windmills

8. Bradford-on-Avon
9. Brinkworth
10. Chiseldon
11. Devizes
12. West Gomeldon, Idmiston
13. East Knoyle
14. Wilton

Windpumps

15. Broad Hinton
16. Crudwell
17. Steeple Ashton
18. Wilsford
19. Winterslow
20. Wylye
21. Wylye

Watermills

22. Avoncliff Weir and Mills
23. Hazeland Mill
24. Blacklands Mill
25. Drewitts Mill
26. Baldham Mill
27. Seend Head Mill
28. Littleton Mill
29. Rowde Mill
30. Elcott Mill
31. Durnford Mill
32. Marden Mill
33. Coombe Mill
34. Downton Mills
35. Salisbury Mills
36. Harnham Mill
37. South Newton Mill
38. Bishopstrow Mill
39. Sutton Mandeville Mill
40. Tisbury Mill
41. Manor Farm Mill, Winterbourne Gunner
42. Stourhead Gardens, pumping wheels
43. Fox Mill, Purton

Steam, Gas and Electricity

44. Crofton Pumps

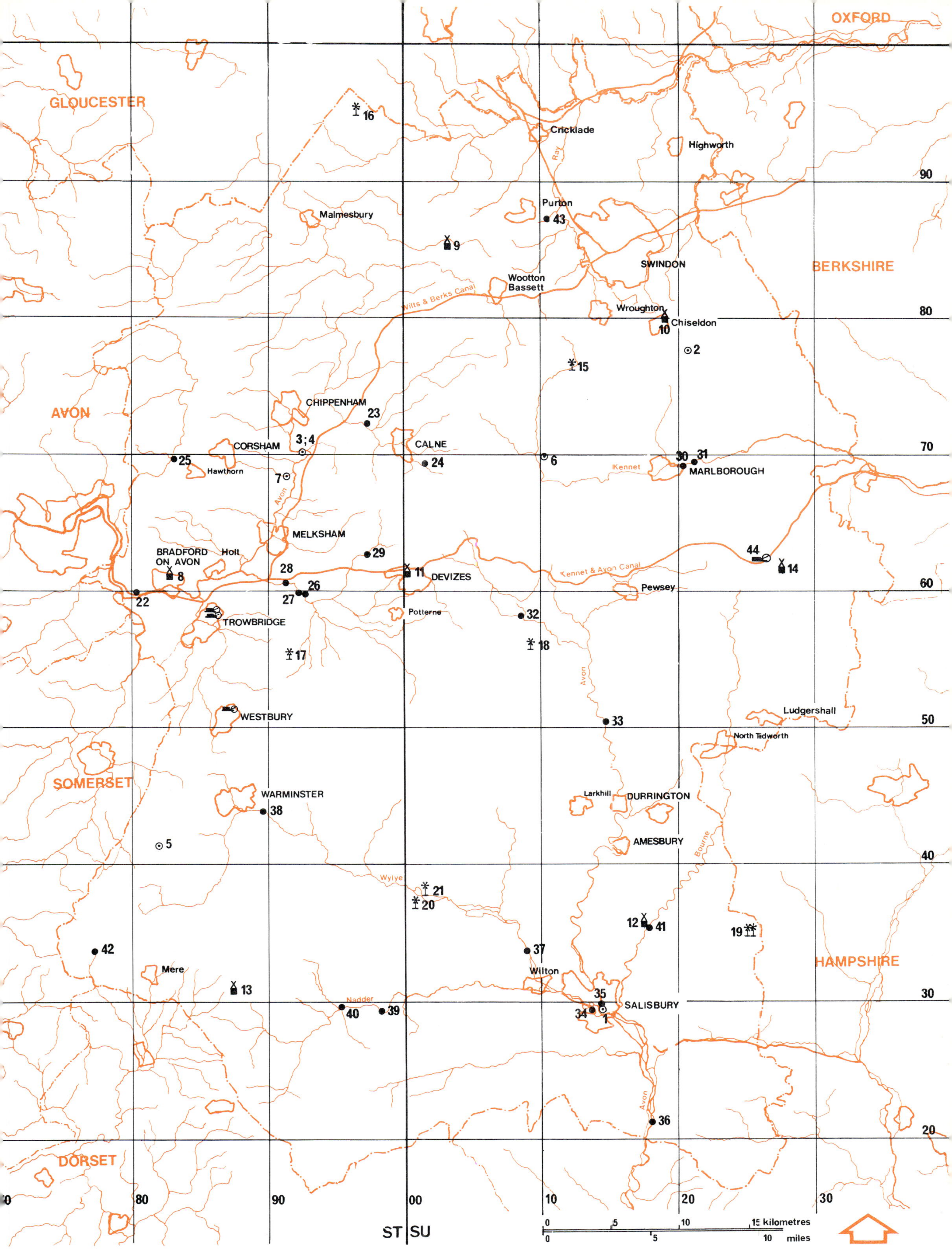

POWER

⊙ animal
windmill
windpump
● water
steam

Horningsham: Manor Farm, barn with apsidal projection formerly housing animal-powered machinery

Crudwell: At Chelworth cross roads a wind-damaged, but otherwise complete oil bath type windpump (Photo., J. Sawtell)

Grafton: Wilton Windmill has recently been restored to working condition (Photo., W.C.C.)

Harnham: Harnham Mill is the oldest surviving watermill in the county

Avoncliff: The weir and Old Mill, a former fulling mill

3. TEXTILES

In the 12th century weavers and fullers are known to have been making woollen cloth in Marlborough and Great Bedwyn, but the trade which made Wiltshire part of a major industrial region, and one of the most important textile areas in the world for several centuries, was centred in the west of the county. Its rise in the 14th century was associated partly with national events, such as the manipulation of wool exports in the Hundred Years War, and partly with a technological innovation, the fulling mill. Fulling is the process by which woollen cloth is felted together after it comes from the loom, and from time immemorial had been carried out by treading on the cloth for many hours in water and fuller's earth, the process which gives rise to our surname Walker.

In the 12th century we first hear of fulling mills, in which water-power was used to drive heavy wooden hammers, called stocks, which pounded the cloth. Some of the earliest known sites of such mills are in Wiltshire, and when the industry began to expand the necessity to find sites where corn mills could be converted for fulling, or new mills built, led to the widespread diffusion of the industry in the valley of the Bristol Avon and its tributaries, and in the Valley of the Wylye from its source down to and including Salisbury. By 1400 Salisbury, already a major commercial city, was also the centre of an important cloth industry, and such small towns as Bradford, Trowbridge, Westbury, Steeple Ashton and Castle Combe were the homes of prosperous clothiers. Evidence of this can be seen in some of the fine churches of the area, of which Steeple Ashton is an outstanding example.

Of the many fulling mills which can be traced from documentary sources, only one early example remains, at West Harnham, near Salisbury, dating from *c.* 1500. Other sites are now occupied by comparatively late buildings of which an excellent example is the mill at Stowford on the Somerset border adjoining the road from Trowbridge to Farleigh Hungerford. It dates from the later 18th century, and was used as a fulling mill until the 1840s. Nearby are a large 16th century house in which the successive clothiers on the site lived, and a building which was probably built as a mill also in the 16th century, now a house.

Apart from the fulling mill the medieval textile industry had no distinctive industrial building. The clothier, who in this area generally owned the material through all the processes from raw wool to finished cloth, sometimes lives at his mill, or sometimes in a town or village where he organised his trade from his own house. The house called Talboys at Keevil is a good example of a clothier's house of the late 16th century. At such a house the clothier would store his wool, distribute it for spinning and weaving, and despatch it to market when it had come back from the mill. The main manufacturing processes were carried out in the homes of his workpeople. For some types of cloth, especially those made at Salisbury, there were elaborate finishing processes in which the nap on the cloth was raised by using teazles (the special hard fuller's teazle, *dipsacus fullonum*, and then sheared off using the immense iron shears of which a pair can be seen in the Garlick Museum at Trowbridge. But much cloth was exported unfinished to Flanders and Italy.

In the early 17th century an important change in the product of the industry took place. The new cloths were called medleys, because they were made by mixing wool dyed two or more colours before spinning, or Spanish cloths, because they were made partly, or in the best qualities wholly, of fine wool imported from Spain. They were much lighter than the clothiers formerly produced, and were finished locally, often by specialised craftsmen called clothworkers who worked on commission from the clothiers. The prosperity of the clothiers who produced this cloth in the 17th and 18th centuries, has left a notable impress on the towns of the west of Wiltshire, where it may almost be assumed that any house of the period of any pretension was built by a clothier. The quality of some at Trowbridge so impressed Sir Nikolaus Pevsner that he compared them to the *palazzi* of Verona. The best group is the Parade, now used as offices by Watney-Mann (West), among them the beautifully decorated stone façade of Parade House of *c.* 1730. Nearby Lloyd's Bank occupies a stately house of about the same date. Bradford, Chippenham and Warminster all contain houses of equal grandeur. On the outskirts of Bradford stands Belcombe Court, built for the Yerbury family in the 1720s and 30s, partly by John Wood the elder, the Bath architect, from which they carried on their clothing business for many years.

Though the clothiers' houses present a grand front to the street, at the back they often present a more utilitarian aspect. We know from documentary sources that many were used partly as workshops and storerooms, and that others had workshops built adjoining them or in their gardens. These remains are often difficult to see from the street. Adjoining Courtfield House, Polebarn Road, Trowbridge, on the west, is a good example of a clothier's workshop of the 1760s, and long windows to let in ample light for some processes can be seen on the east side of the main house. Much has been written about weavers' houses in the district, especially connected with those Flemings who are so popularly associated with the industry but who have proved so elusive to serious research. The foreign influence on the local trade was almost entirely confined to a small and well-documented immigration to Trowbridge and Bradford in the 1670s. As with the clothiers' houses, it would not be far from true to point to any cottage in West Wiltshire over 150 years old and guess that at some time or other it held a loom. Spinning was done much further afield, providing a means of subsistence for women and children over much of the county. The urban environment of the 17th century worker (at a fairly prosperous level) is best seen at Bradford, where the terraces of Newtown, Middle Rank and Tory rising up the hill represent the expansion of the town in the prosperous period after *c.* 1660. Many were probably occupied by clothworkers.

So far we have been referring to an industry whose only distinctive industrial buildings were the fulling mill and the workshop attached to the clothier's house.

Apart from fulling the processes were carried out by hand tools or on simple machines like the loom and the spinning wheel. A fundamental change came with the introduction of machinery from about 1790 onwards. The earliest machines were for carding, spinning, raising and shearing, and their introduction caused intermittent industrial trouble among the workpeople. Early machines were small; some, such as the spinning jenny, were driven by the operator, and others could be turned by manpower, or by using horses, generally by gearing from a vertical shaft turned by two or three horses walking in a circle. Some workshops were built for machinery driven in these ways. The largest and earliest, probably built for jennies, is at the corner of Snuff Street and New Park Street in Devizes, dated 1785, and bearing the initials of John Anstie. Another dated example, of 1816, adjoins the Linnet public house at Great Hinton.

Almost immediately, however, the clothiers turned to water power to drive the heavier carding machines, and the 1790s saw a spate of factory building on the rivers of West Wiltshire (Salisbury was by this time in full decline as a textile centre). Sometimes fulling or corn mills could be acquired and added to, or replaced; just occasionally a clothier could find a site where he could build a new mill without damaging the rights of the mills above and below. The first reference so far found to driving the new machinery by water-power comes from Avoncliff, just below Bradford, in 1791, when a boy was killed by the mainshaft of the mill. Part of the factory remains on the south side of the river there, where it replaced a long-standing fulling mill. At the other end of the great stone weir is a 19th century fulling mill with its large iron breastshot wheel with paddles still in position.

Probably equally early is Avon Mill, Malmesbury. The earlier corn mill on the site was bought by a Bradford clothier in 1790, with the intention of moving his trade to a place where the industry had been extinct for some time, so that he could avoid labour troubles when introducing machinery. His graceful stone mill must be one of the earliest surviving textile factories in the world. The tall narrow building is lighted by long ranges of windows on each of its five storeys to get maximum natural light. Other good water-factories remain in Greenland Mill, Bradford, built by 1884 and Quemerford Mill, adjoining the London road just east of Calne, of unknown date but probably of the 1790s. Others have gone, among them Kingston Mill, Bradford, built *c.* 1807 and demolished in 1972, while of the largest of all, Staverton Factory, built in 1800, only the two lowest floors survive as part of the Nestlés factory there.

Compared with the north, the advent of steam power was delayed by some years in Wiltshire as in all the western clothing districts. The crucial factor was the availability of coal, and especially of canal transport to carry it. The building of the first known engine, at Trowbridge in 1805, took place in the same year as the opening of the Somerset Coal Canal in a satisfactory form. This engine was a small one used to replace horses, and many of the earliest engines were similarly fitted to former horse-driven workshops. Others were fitted to water-driven factories, where they avoided the necessity of the long waiting for a head of water to build up to which many factories had been subject. Good examples of extra parts added to water-driven factories on the addition of a steam engine may be seen at Quemerford Mill near Calne and at Stone Mill, Court Street, Trowbridge, where engines were added to earlier factories in 1814 and 1819 respectively.

The advantages of steam engines were, however, so obvious, that almost immediately, special factories designed from the first to be steam driven were built. Angel Mill at Westbury, of 1806 is the earliest known, still surviving in its original form although surrounded by later additions. Its brick façade is distinguished by a pediment and by rows of segment-headed, stone-framed windows of two lights separated by a stone mullion, a design which became almost *de rigeur* among the factory buildings of the period. At Court Street in Trowbridge can be seen Brick Mill, of 1816, in the same style, and a smaller building is nearby at Cradle Bridge Mill. Two exceptionally interesting early steam factories at Trowbridge, Bridge Mill of *c.* 1807 and Courts Mill of 1812, have been demolished in recent years.

The spate of factory building stopped *c.* 1820, and subsequent years witnessed a very difficult period. Bradford especially suffered a depression which saw almost every firm out of business in 1841, and only in Trowbridge was a certain prosperity maintained. Castle Factory, Court Street, of 1828–1836 is the best example of the middle period of factory building, still with standard stone windows in a brick façade, but with elaborate treatment of the roof at each end, the walls being cut off to meet the half-hipped roof.

The final period of factory building is associated with the last really prosperous period of the industry *c.* 1855–1880. The principal buildings of this are noticeably different in design. Gas was now available for lighting, so that there was no need to adhere to the long narrow plan of earlier times, and the squarer rooms that this made possible could accommodate larger machinery such as the mule. Windows became larger, and the designs of the buildings somewhat more fanciful. The handsomest of these late factories is Abbey Mill at Bradford, built 1874, where the slightly pointed windows are separated by pilasters brought up into arches over the top floor windows, and surmounted by a machicolated parapet. Ashton Mill, near the Park, Trowbridge, is a somewhat plainer building of 1860, and Studley Mill and Innox Mill, both near the Town Bridge there, represent the same idiom in brick.

It was during this last period of prosperity that weaving was finally brought into the factories. A good example of the large single-storey weaving sheds of the period is at Ashton Mill, Trowbridge (now K.A.M.) built 1860. Some hand-loom weaving survived into the seventies in villages such as Dilton Marsh, a place which had originated in the 18th century by people squatting on common land. In the village some loom shops, single-storeyed buildings attached to houses, can be seen; while at Chapmanslade there are two three-storeyed weaving shops (one dated 1821) now a pair of houses, which would have held a number of looms.

Other weavers had looms in the main rooms of their houses. A terrace of two-storeyed stone houses on the west of Trowbridge Road in Bradford each contained a shop for two looms when advertised in 1823. Probably because it specialised in narrow cloth, Trowbridge contained a number of terraces of three-storeyed houses built between 1790 and 1830 in which the top floor housed the looms. Many have been demolished in recent years, but good examples of the 1790s can be seen at Yerbury Street and Newtown.

One later example of workpeople's housing should be mentioned. In 1869 Abraham Laverton, Liberal cloth manufacturer of Westbury, was defeated by his Conservative opponent Phipps in two fiercely contested elections (the first annulled for corruption) for the borough of Westbury. Many of Laverton's workpeople, he claimed, were ejected by Phipps for voting for their master, who in 1869 built a spacious layout of 39 houses called Prospect Square, for them to live in. This is still intact south of the Bratton road.

The fate of the fulling mills should be mentioned. In 1833 John Dyer, a Trowbridge engineer, invented the rotary fulling machine still widely used today, and the stocks were gradually superseded. Nevertheless the last mills survived almost to the end of the 19th century.

Some of the ancillary buildings of the industry have survived. Several wool drying stoves—small stone towers in which the wool was dried by the heat of a stove after scouring—remain, at Bearfield in Bradford, Horningsham, and at Lowbourne and Church Street in Melksham. A later building of brick is at Ashton Mill, Trowbridge. On a small stone bridge over the Biss at Trowbridge, a few yards upstream from the Town Bridge stands a building of perforated brickwork, the only local example left of a handle house. In this, teazles, damp from use on the wet cloth, were dried by a current of air. At Studley Mills nearby is a good example of a 'prestige' office block of 1878; others can be seen at 4–5 Fore Street, Trowbridge and Greenland Mill, Bradford.

The industry is still active in one factory at Trowbridge. Its products from 1699 onwards can be seen in pattern books kept by several Trowbridge and Westbury firms at the County Record Office in Trowbridge.

Other textile trades were carried on in Wiltshire in the past. Silk weaving can be traced in the county from the 17th century, but a more important silk industry flourished at several places in the 19th century in factories formerly used for woollens. The largest were at Malmesbury (the factory still standing by the bridge), Chippenham, Devizes and Crockerton.

The district round Mere had an extensive linen industry in the 18th century, making especially bed-ticking, that is the material in which flock beds were encased. This was mainly a cottage industry, but spinning by water-power was introduced in 1837. Lordsmead Mill at Mere is a good example of the small factories where this was done. The industry died out in the late 19th century.

At Aldbourne, fustians, cloths made of a mixture of linen and cotton yarn, were produced from the 17th century to about 1850, and lace was made at Downton and Malmesbury. Two old established textile industries are still carried on at Wilton—the making of the famous carpets begun by the middle of the 18th century, and of high quality felt for a variety of industrial purposes.

Gazetteer

For Trowbridge sites see separate map page

Fulling Mills

1. West Harnham
2. Stowford
3. Avoncliff (north side)

Clothiers' Houses

4. Talboys, Keevil
5. Belcombe House, Bradford-on-Avon

Cloth Workers' Houses

6. Newtown, Middle Rank and Tory, Bradford-on-Avon
7. Prospect Square, Westbury

Factories

8. Ansties Mill, Devizes
9. Great Hinton

Water

10. Avoncliff (south side)
11. Avon Mill, Malmesbury
12. Greenland Mill, Bradford-on-Avon
13. Staverton Factory

Water/Steam

14. Quemerford Mill

Steam

15. Angel Mill, Westbury
16. Abbey Mill, Bradford-on-Avon

Hand Loom Shops

17. Dilton Marsh
18. Chapmanslade
19. Trowbridge Road, Bradford-on-Avon

Wool Drying Stoves

20. Bearfield, Bradford-on-Avon
21. Horningsham
22. Lowbourne, Melksham
23. Church Street, Melksham

Office Blocks

24. Greenland Mill, Bradford-on-Avon

Miscellaneous

25. Wilton Carpet Factory
26. Lordsmead Linen Factory, Mere

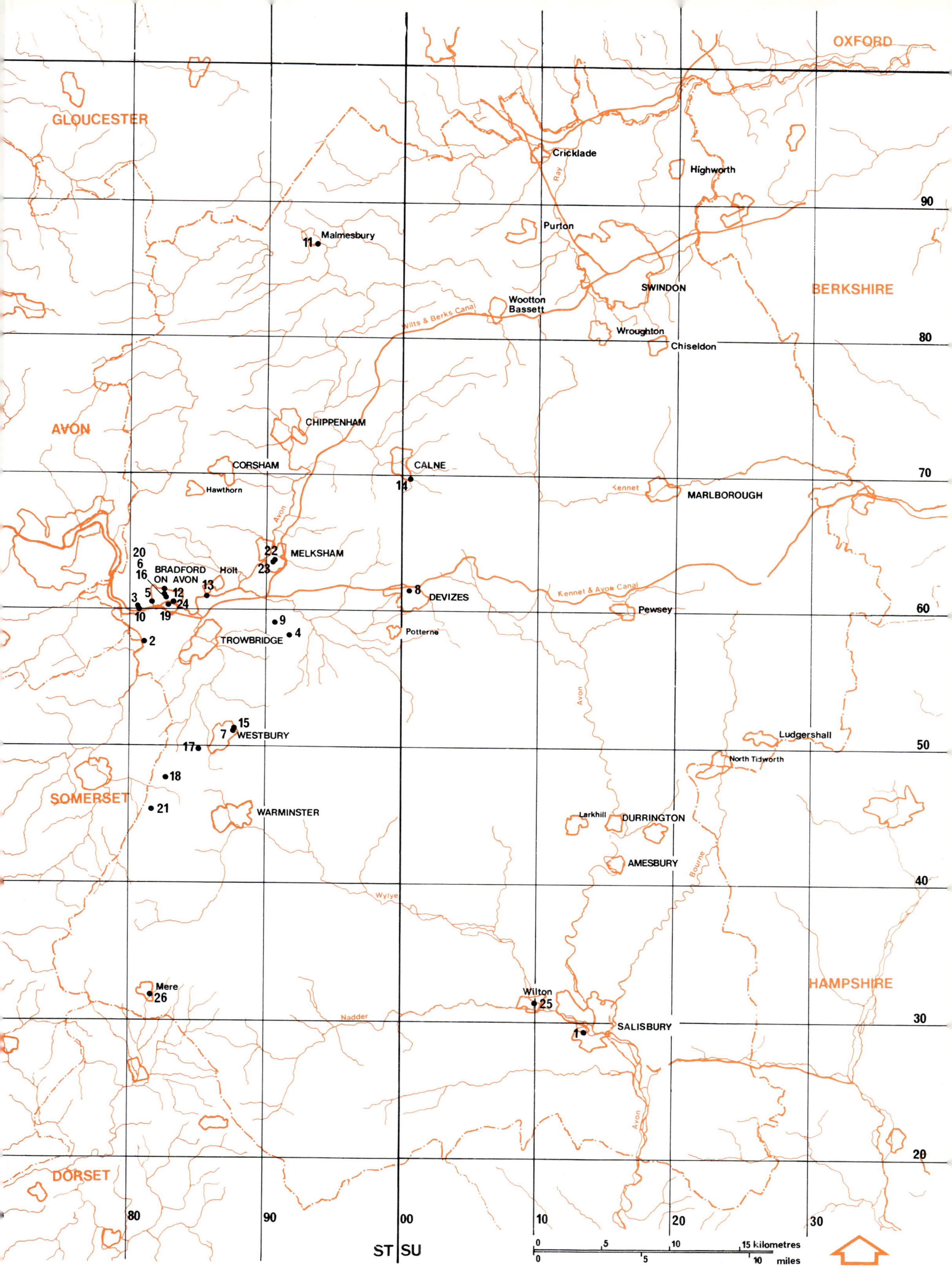

OXFORD
GLOUCESTER
Cricklade
Highworth
Purton
Malmesbury
SWINDON
BERKSHIRE
Wootton Bassett
Wilts & Berks Canal
Wroughton
Chiseldon
AVON
CHIPPENHAM
CORSHAM
CALNE
Hawthorn
MARLBOROUGH
Kennet
MELKSHAM
BRADFORD ON AVON
Holt
DEVIZES
Kennet & Avon Canal
Pewsey
TROWBRIDGE
Potterne
WESTBURY
Ludgershall
North Tidworth
SOMERSET
WARMINSTER
Larkhill
DURRINGTON
AMESBURY
Bourne
Wylye
HAMPSHIRE
Mere
Wilton
Nadder
SALISBURY
DORSET
ST SU
15 kilometres
10 miles

TEXTILES

Bradford-on-Avon: Greenland Mill

Trowbridge: Castle Mill

Malmesbury: Avon Mill

Melksham: Wool drying stove in Church Street

4. QUARRIES AND BUILDING MATERIALS

The quality of Wiltshire's rocks for building varies greatly across the county; in the north-west good limestone abounds, on the south-east side the stone belt is overlain by clays, many suitable for brick making. Then follow the Gault Clay, the Greensands and the chalk. Until transport of bricks became easy the buildings of the Chalklands had to resort to cob and flint, with thatch for the roofs. That simple pattern is partly interrupted at Swindon where Portland and Purbeck Stone outcrop; the same rocks occur in the Vale of Wardour.

Cotswold Limestones

Oolitic limestone, typical of the Cotswolds, outcrops from Bradford-on-Avon in a north-north-east direction until it passes out of the county north of Malmesbury (as shown on the map). The rocks vary in lithology fairly rapidly; from Bradford to Bath and Box is the famous Bath Stone which is limestone free of fossils and which can thus be cut freely in any direction without fear of a split in an unwanted direction. For this reason the stone is termed 'freestone'. The freestone quality quickly disappears, and more irregular bedded limestone is found elsewhere. The freestone lies between two limestones of inferior quality known by the quarrymen as 'Rags'. The Lower Rags consist of a coarse shelly limestone and the Upper vary from a clay limestone to another shelly limestone; the freestone thickness is about 2–3 m (6–9 ft).

The term Bath Stone covers several variations according to quarry location. The stone from Box is called Hazelbury or Box Ground; that from Limpley Stoke, Stoke Ground, and nearer to Bath in Avon is Combe Down and Hampton Down. Some resist decay better than others and most of them turn black in smoky atmospheres. The stone is soft and easy to work when it first comes out of the quarry and thus the stone masons were able to make spheres and the circular shapes popular for balustrades.

The Romans clearly used much of the best stone for the town of Aquae Sulis; they probably worked into the sides of the numerous hillsides, mining underground for a limited distance. The Anglo-Saxons in the 7th century used Box Ground for St. Laurence Chapel in Bradford-on-Avon. In 1222 Bath Stone was used for the piers of the great hall of Winchester Castle, but otherwise in the middle ages Hazelbury stone went to more local monastic buildings—Lacock Abbey, Monkton Farleigh Priory and later to Great Chalfield and Longleat House. About 1740, Ralph Allen developed quarries, mainly at Bath, on a much larger scale and Wood built the 'palace' of Prior Park to advertise the magnificence of Bath Stone. At the beginning of the 19th century John Nash extended the fame of Bath Stone to London. Unfortunately, as mentioned above, the stone decayed in London's sooty atmosphere and Portland Stone had to replace it or cover it up. A large influence in the extended fame of the stone was due to the new ease of transport, first by the Kennet and Avon Canal and then by the Great Western Railway.

During the construction of Box Tunnel in 1841, more valuable building stone was revealed. This led to a network of underground quarries in the direction of Corsham. By 1862, there were 8 km (5 miles) of tunnels and tramways. In 1887 the various separate firms were united as Bath Stone Firms Ltd., and in the first year their output was 42,480 m^3 ($1\frac{1}{2}$ million cubic feet) of stone; by 1900 output was 84,960 m^3 (3 million cubic feet) and the roadways were thought to extend to 96 km (60 miles).

Box Hill (ST 835 695)

To climb up from Box to the village of Box Hill and find the Quarryman's Arms is to enter a world of past centuries. At various points further back, below the plateau, will be found the boarded entrances to the mines, formerly called East Gate, North Gate and West Gate.

To prevent collapse of the roof above the quarries much valuable freestone had to be left as pillars. With the use of modern equipment an operation has been in progress since 1968 whereby a stone quarrying company aims to obtain the freestone of the remaining pillars from above.

Corsham—Monk's Park (ST 878 683)

As mentioned above, the underground workings started in the Corsham area following the Box Tunnel excavation. Of these only one remains in operation today and it is possible by arrangement to see not only the modern methods but a demonstration of how the stone was prised out during the last century. One can only marvel at the patience and ingenuity of those who extracted the stone blocks without any power-driven tools. The stone is kept underground until May because the 'green' stone is damaged by frost. So extensive were the underground workings in the Corsham region that the Air Ministry took over the disused galleries for the storage of ammunition and in 1942 a large aircraft factory was built underground.

The actual process of quarrying or 'getting' the stone is well described in *The Builder* of April 20th, 1895. Two methods prevailed, either open quarrying such as was practiced at Murhill, or underground quarrying, the more usual method.

In open quarrying the overburden was removed by shotblasting, and the rubble heaped behind the working face leaving a space for carts to transport the worked stone. The building stone itself was removed by cutting with a single-handed saw down to the bedding plane at right angles to the face, a second cut at right angles to this was made, and the stone block removed from its bed by wedges and levers. The rough surfaces were squared by the use of a two-edged stone axe. Before the advent of the single-handed saw in the last century picks were used to remove the stone, a process which was far more wasteful of the stone.

For underground quarrying mines were opened in three different ways; by driving a horizontal tunnel directly into a cliff or hillside; by constructing steeply inclined tunnels, and rarely by vertical shafts. An example of the latter method is the 'Cathedral', a vertical shaft sunk to reach the stone where it widened out to form a bell-shaped cavern. The stone was removed by means of a chain and horse gin, an early date for the working is indicated by the pick marks on the walls.

In getting stone from mines, first two or three inches of stone under the roof were removed, this is termed the picking jad; a further thin bed, the picking bed, is removed below this, these operations carried out using picks with handles of increasing lengths to work back from the face. In the space so made a single-handed saw was inserted and the block sawn down to the bedding plane using water as a lubricant to wash away the stone dust. Finally, using iron bars and the crane always erected at the working face, the block was broken from its bed. When carrying out this operation the quarryman stood upon the picking standing. Many of the cranes survive, in form, a substantial timber upright socketed into the floor and roof of the passage, a wooden jib mounted on to the upright and the crane worked by a handle mounted on to a large, toothed wheel engaging a smaller wheel and giving the low ratio necessary to move large blocks. On some cranes a dual gearing was obtained by means of a sliding shaft.

The stone was removed from the mines to the railway by means of tramroads, however, at the Corsham Down Quarry the stone was loaded directly on to railway trucks. At Clift Quarry the trucks were drawn out by means of a steam engine on the level, while at Park Lane Quarry the trucks were hauled up the incline to the summit of a low ridge then allowed to run under gravity to Corsham Railway Station. A brakeman was in charge of each truck and a horse was available to give occasional assistance. Tramroad remains and the slots left by sleepers survive in the passages.

The stone quarried in winter should properly be left underground until the weather becomes milder, then allowed to season on the surface through the summer; in this way the stone is less liable to decay. The unprecedented demand for the stone in the latter half of the 19th century led to its being used without weathering with disastrous results and a subsequent maligning of its suitability.

Bradford-on-Avon

The Bath Stone continues from Box in a southerly direction as far as Bradford where it is suddenly replaced by the Bradford Clay. There are remnants of former large open workings in the Winsley area, for example, at Murhill (ST 795 607).

In Bradford itself the quarries went underground into the sides of the hills. Some years ago the disused caves were taken over by the Agaric mushroom growing firm since the caves provide ideal conditions, darkness, the desired humidity and a constant temperature.

Leigh Delamere (ST 892 793)

In addition to the large underground mines there are numerous small quarries for local building stone to be found right across the Stone Belt from Bradford-on-Avon to Malmesbury. From them the more massive blocks were used for the walls of cottages, the very thin slabs for their roofs and the remainder for the stone walls so characteristic of the north-western part of the county. One such former quarry east of Leigh Delamere forms the back of the picnic area of the filling station on the M4.

Stone Tile Roofs

The most characteristic feature of Cotswold houses and cottages is their stone roof. The best quality tiles came from Stonesfield in Oxfordshire but one cannot imagine the local builder paying for the long distance transport; instead he would find suitable seams of thin bedded limestone in quarries as mentioned above. The grassy hollow just west of the road south of Gastard (ST 882 676) marks the site of one former industry.

Corallian Stone

This formation is basically a limestone with fossil corals at certain levels. It lies between the Oxford and Kimmeridge Clays and thus extends the region of natural stone buildings further to the south-east. Much use was made in former times of the Coral Rag division; as the name implies the rock has an irregular nature; it has proved to be a durable building stone provided a generous amount of mortar is used. The best quality stone was called the Calne Freestone. Under close inspection it is seen to be composed of large oolitic grains and small shell fragments. The principal quarry was beside the former workhouse and acquired the name 'Workhouse Quarry'; its remains now form part of the grounds of St. Mary's School. The Corallian outcrop continues north-east from Calne towards Wootton Bassett and numerous small quarries were dug out in the area around Lyneham.

Portland and Purbeck Stone

The village of Chilmark has acquired fame by virtue of the building stone which was quarried from the sides of a small valley known as the Chilmark Ravine. Chilmark Stone is a fine-grained sandy limestone, creamy white when fresh but grey when weathered.

The stone was extracted from underground mines mainly on the west side of the valley and was used for the cathedrals both of Old Sarum and Salisbury and even as far away as Rochester. In 1938 all the quarries were taken over by the War Department for the storage of ammunition and they still remain closed to the public.

Stone from the same geological horizon on the Isle of Portland was not worked until the end of the 17th century when it was chosen by Wren for his London churches. The Portland Stone, as it became known, travelled by sea to London and elsewhere, which was a great advantage over road at the time. During the 19th century because of the lack of access to good transportation Wardour Portland Stone became limited to local buildings. The various buildings on the Fonthill estates took a large amount of stone from underground workings near the Fonthill lake (ST 934 316). They are now protected by grilles which allow only the bats to use the caves. Of the numerous other quarries in the

Vale a former one south of the railway crossing at Chicksgrove has now been destroyed by the large excavations for Portland Stone that is crushed for road metal (ST 964 296). West of Tisbury (ST 935 291) is a small quarry which until recently had a quarryman's crane and stonemason's workshop. Close to the quarry is a lime kiln in which the waste stone was fired to produce quick lime. Such kilns were commonly associated with limestone quarries; at Teffont Evias a tram-road ran from the quarry (ST 991 311) to a kiln which has recently been restored (ST 899 313).

Swindon

As the result of a small syncline Portland and Purbeck beds crop up on the hill of Old Swindon. Some very good building stone lies below a sandy bed and was quarried at several points on the hill. The best known of these was the Okus Quarry near Okus Road (ST 147 836). For many years Messrs. Bradley extracted sand and the building stone. The quarry, on being closed in the 1960s, was listed as a Site of Special Scientific Interest and a small section was preserved by the Wiltshire County Council and the Swindon Education Authority. Nevertheless it is rather a poor remnant of the former quarry face. Not far away is Town Garden (ST 151 833) an open space created by the removal of a very large volume of Purbeck rocks above Portland Stone. Useful geological sections are still available for study around the boundary rock faces. The Wilts and Berks Canal and later the G.W.R. were able to transport the Swindon stone to other areas but probably most of it went to build the Old Swindon houses while the Victorian New Swindon is built of brick from the clay pits to the north.

Chalk and Flint

Chalk is a special form of limestone, being almost pure calcium carbonate; it is a porous, uncemented and generally soft rock. Two harder bands however occur at different levels, the Melbourn Rock and the Chalk Rock.

Whereas at Beer in Devonshire chalk is mined as a building stone, neither of the hard layers of Wiltshire can be used for external structures; however many walls of older cottages were built of chalk boulders and the inside wall of Wanborough church consists of chalk. On Salisbury Plain where building materials were scarce chalk was used in several ways. For cob, powdered chalk was mixed with clay, manure and water; the mixture was trodden and left to dry. No shuttering was used and each layer had to harden before the next was added, so the walls were broad and as far as possible corners were avoided. Cob cottages can therefore be recognised by their round walls. For pugged walls a mixture of chalk, mud and water was poured between shuttering and rammed firm. Walls whether of cob or pugged chalk had to be protected from damp rising from below and falling as rain from above. The walls therefore had some stone foundation and a thatch covering which gives an attractive finish. Another alternative was to use the chalk mixture between a wood framework in what is known as wattle and daub. Laths or wattles were fixed at the back of the wood frames and the chalk-clay mix was daubed on to the laths, given a plane finish and covered with lime-plaster which could be white or coloured.

The Upper Chalk which underlies nearly all of Salisbury Plain contains numerous bands of flint, an almost indestructible mass of silica. All arable fields are covered with flints and farmers would have to remove the larger ones which could then be used for wall structures. The flints were used in various ways as can be observed in the houses and churches during a journey through the villages. Occasionally they are used untreated and set in a generous layer of mortar. More often they are split approximately in half or knapped and set so that the irregular shape faces inwards and the plane dressed surface outwards. When the cross section shape can be rectangular a very neat wall is obtained. It is rare however that a whole wall is built entirely of flint; two decorative patterns, which also help the strength of the wall, were evolved in Wiltshire. Firstly banded brick and flint in which a few layers of flint,then two courses of brick are set and then followed by another layer of flint and so on; alternatively a chequered pattern is achieved by arranging alternative rectangles of flint and stone. For the latter, ashlared stone is used to provide just a facing of rectangular shape rather than a complete block. For buildings on Salisbury Plain, Portland Stone was the common choice because it was near at hand from the Vale of Wardour. Many houses in Chitterne are good examples of the chequered use of flint, the church of Berwick St. James is another.

The remnants of small quarries dug at the levels both of the Melbourn and Chalk Rock can be found at many places where those layers crop out, mainly along the north facing scarp of the Plain and on the Marlborough Downs. The larger chalk quarries have resulted from the extraction of chalk for its other uses.

Chalk for Lime

Quick lime was made from chalk in lime kilns and as already mentioned from scrap limestone. Together with sand, quick lime was formerly the necessary ingredient of mortar, but since the production of Portland Cement, the lime kiln has almost disappeared. However, numerous lime works are marked on the older maps. The former large quarry at Ogbourne St. George (SU 207 739) was one and another was half way up the hill below part of the Warminster golf course (ST 876 461).

'Lime' in the form of calcium carbonate is required for agricultural use especially on acid soils. The large chalk quarry at West Harnham (SU 128 288) has been cut back over the years and worked at three levels. The crushing plant was set up on the middle level so that the powdered chalk could be delivered into trucks at the lower level. Another quarry developed in the same way at two levels is on Charnage Down (ST 846 335). A recent addition is a quarry just off the Salisbury-Southampton road at SU 217 243. The technique now differs, very heavy machines move slowly over an even surface and just scrape the chalk off that surface.

Another important use of chalk is in the very pure and fine form known as whiting. The quarry at Quidhampton (ST 112 314) is owned by Messrs. Rogers and Cooke and their product goes to a large range of industries.

Sandstone and Sand

Wiltshire has no sandstone like the Pennant Sandstone of the Bristol area that is suitable for a whole building. Wiltshire's sandstones include the Lower Calcareous Grit, Lower and Upper Greensands, some Eocene Sands south of Salisbury and the Sarsens of Marlborough Downs. The Lower Greensand often contains ironstone boulders as can be seen at Naish Hill Sand Pit (ST 939 693). From other quarries in that district sufficient boulders were collected to build most of the cottages in Sandy Lane, and they then had thatched roofs. The village is a unique example of a uniform pattern of cottage construction. The Upper Greensand also contains bands of harder boulders at a few levels but the only example deserving the name of building stone was the Potterne Stone which mostly came from a small quarry behind Plank's Dairy in Coxhill Lane (ST 998 584).

The odd Upper Greensand boulders did find a function for an interesting feature of the old houses in the neighbourhood in their use for the foundations and lower parts of houses of brick and other materials. The sand boulders were found to transmit less moisture from the ground than brick and thus acted as a form of damp course.

Sarsen Stones

This unique rock found mainly on the Marlborough Downs should be included as a sandstone. It is generally agreed that when a deposit of sand was laid down over the clays which first covered the chalk in the post-chalk era, the sand grains were later cemented by silica thus forming a very durable rock known as quartzite. When erosion later removed the softer clays, the quartzite boulders, later to be called sarsens, were left strewn over the downs. The sarsen blocks were then liable to be moved by various agents; the rapid torrents from melt water, following any rapid thaw during the periglacial conditions of an ice age, would have carried many blocks from higher to lower ground. Then early man moved many to Avebury and Stonehenge and later in Romano-British times they were used for the foundation of houses but it was in the Medieval period that sarsens were frequently used for building; they were crudely split by heating them on a fire and pouring on cold water. Some were found to split naturally into rough rectangular shapes.

About 1850 Edward Free moved from the Chiltern Hills area to Fyfield and set up as a sarsen stonemason. In the High Wycombe area he had developed an advanced technique for cutting sarsens more or less to size. In 1890 the Free family moved to Marlborough and Edward's son continued the business.

When barges on the Kennet and Avon Canal brought coal from Somerset to the Vale of Pewsey, the Free family would collect the coal and load the barges with sarsens for the return journey. Sarsens were also found to be ideal for tramway setts when tramways were introduced to Swindon and also for roadside kerbstones. During the early part of this century the Frees' output would have been 300 tonnes a year. So fast were the sarsens disappearing that various bodies including the National Trust, the Wiltshire Archaeological and Natural History Society and Marlborough College raised £600 to purchase Piggledene, Lockeridge Dene and a large area of Fyfield Down to conserve the remaining sarsens there.

Sand

Sand is an essential constituent of builders' mix for mortar. The sand grains must be sharp, that is angular. Sand from the Upper Greensand is not satisfactory but the following are or have been sources:

Sahara Sand Pit (ST 939 648)
The pit was first opened in 1937 and reopened by Mr. Freeman in 1949 with the installation of screening machinery; however disaster befell a profitable business in 1960 when water which started to seep into the quarry from the sides and floor eventually drowned the machinery to a depth of 3.5 m (12 ft). The quarry is now dry but no longer worked.

The Sands, Calne (SU 014 713)
This pit has been worked by Messrs. Bradley and Sons since 1928 starting in a small way. Today the machinery must be much the same as that of 50 years ago; men would have dug out the sand and taken it to the conveyor belt which at the other end tipped it into the washing plant. As the sand supply was found further and further from the plant, the conveyor belt was increased in length so that it is now 0.8 km (½ mile) long and fed from mechanical diggers. Since the Lower Greensand overlies Gault Clay all the sand pits become filled with water which could be useful in conditions of drought.

High Penn Sand Pit (SU 015 728)
Not far away to the north-west this pit is in Lower Greensand and is owned by Messrs. Hill of Swindon. It is extensive and is worked along the same lines as that of Bradleys. The sand is supplied not only for builders but also for the production of asphalt.

Clay Pits

There are four possible clay deposits available for Wiltshire bricks, the Oxford, the Kimmeridge, the Gault and the London Clays. The most popular was the Gault and the least the Kimmeridge. If bricks are made entirely of plastic clay, they warp in the kiln; to prevent this the clay is mixed with some sand. However, the Gault as at Devizes has natural sandy clay bands with some iron content at certain levels.

The Devizes clay therefore produced a non-warping brick with a good red colour as the result of the iron oxides. The Caen Hill pit (ST 982 613) was opened soon after 1810 when the long flight of locks was constructed for the canal and revealed the outcrop of Gault. About two million bricks were supplied and taken down the canal to build the canal tunnel at Savernake. The Devizes Brick and Tile Works was owned for many years by Mr. R. B. Mullings (1845–1910) and in more recent years by Mr. Oram of Devizes.

The works were closed a few years ago and the site is now used as a ready-mixed concrete and plant depot. A good idea of the former industry can still be gained by a visit to the site, the kilns were close to the entrance of Caen Hill; the clay was dug during the summer from the east end and laid out to weather under winter rain and frost. The quarry provides the largest exposure of Gault in Wiltshire and, in fact, anywhere to the west of Surrey and Sussex. Formerly there were many other Gault Clay brickworks, a large one at Badbury south of Swindon (SU 190 815) is now used as a depot by the Severn Valley Brick Co. of Avonmouth; a three-chamber, double-ended Newcastle kiln used for firing hand made bricks survives. The Gault has a narrow outcrop at the foot of the Upper Greensand escarpment on the south side of Pewsey Vale; in fact the Gault/Greensand boundary coincides roughly with the railway line. Formerly there was a small brickworks near the site of Lavington Station, the site is now labelled 'Private Fishing'; and a mile to the east another former works is now occupied by Systems and Components Ltd.

The remains of other small brickyards, generally marked by uneven ground, can be seen south of Dauntsey Station, at Crockerton near Warminster, Clarendon Park near Salisbury, and at numerous other sites. The local brick industry provides a good but sad example of the small being swallowed by the large. The vast London Brick Company near Peterborough now has almost the monopoly.

Wiltshire, however, does have one brickworks in active production, namely that at Purton (SU 086 888) in the Oxford Clay which has the advantage of some carbonaceous content which helps the firing of the bricks. The brickyard, now owned by Messrs. Hills of Swindon, was first used about 1890, the present ownership dating from 1906. One other brickyard should be mentioned because it was run on the smallest possible scale, namely by one man, Mr. Tanner. The pit, in loamy London Clay is near Oakridge Wood, Whaddon south of Salisbury (ST 202 261). Mr. Tanner's father started working about 50 years ago; until recently he made 500 bricks a day during the summer and fired them in the kilns during the winter. A bypass has recently been cut through the yard demolishing the Scotch kilns which had a capacity of 40,000 bricks.

Cement and Concrete

In a general way there have been three ages for the use of building materials; firstly the period of natural stone or other natural materials, then that of the artificially made brick and finally the concrete age. Wiltshire, Swindon apart, has almost escaped the concrete erections, however; the county provides the essentials for concrete namely a mixture of chalk and clay for the cement which is mixed with river gravel deposits. Most of the concrete has gone into the foundations of motorways.

Although not an example of industrial archaeology, the Westbury works of the Associated Portland Cement Manufacturers use chalk which is quarried and processed above the town then sent down a pipe line as slurry to the works just alongside the railway (ST 882 527). The site lies on Kimmeridge Clay which is dug out, dried to be mixed with the chalk and some gypsum and heated strongly in a rotary kiln.

Gravel Beds

Before the digging of numerous pits south of the Thames between Ashton Keynes and Cricklade, gravel was obtained from a deposit found below the alluvium of the River Avon when its course was different from the one of today. These deposits lie south of Great Somerford. The screening plant for the gravel was set up at Christian Malford (ST 963 788).

The Thames Gravels are near to the surface and represent relatively more recent deposits from the head waters of the river. When all the available gravel has been removed and the holes filled with water the Cotswold Water Park will be created with facilities for fishing, sailing and some natural waterside habitats.

East Knoyle: Lime kiln beside the road to Hindon

Box: Crane typical of many surviving at former working faces in the quarries. (*Photo., Geoff Roberts*)

Badbury Wick: A three-chambered, double-ended Newcastle Kiln

Westbury: The blast furnaces at the Westbury Iron Works (*Photo., Devizes Museum*)

5. THE IRON INDUSTRY

Iron ore in Wiltshire is associated with the Kimmeridge Clay at Westbury and with the Ferruginous Sands of the Lower Greensand at Seend which also outcrops west and north-west of Devizes and further north near Calne.

Iron has been worked in Wiltshire, probably from the Iron Age. Iron ore and slags have been found at All Cannings Cross, and the hill forts of Lidbury and Casterley. In the Seend–Bromham area ash and slag from smelting operations have been found in association with Romano–British material. The clearest evidence of early smelting has been discovered at Ramsbury where in 1975 three Saxon smelting furnaces were found together with anvil stones and large quantities of slag. In 1294 Edward I granted a lease to the monks of Stanley Abbey to dig and smelt ore on their demesne lands within Chippenham Forest.

In the 17th century Aubrey mentions the iron ore of Seend, which he describes as being of a quality which could be smelted in the forge of the local blacksmith with greater ease than that of the Forest of Dean, which would suggest that it had been used locally for some time.

Commercially the Seend iron works were started in 1856 when a Mr. Holloway, an iron master of Christchurch, purchased the rights to 0.1 hectares (¼ acre) land near the Bell Inn. 20,000 tonnes of ore were extracted and sold for a large profit to the Tredegar Iron Company of South Wales.

A Mr. W. Sarl then obtained rights to work the surrounding land. A tramway was constructed to the Kennet and Avon Canal and operations commenced in 1857. The ore was shipped to iron works in Wales and Staffordshire. The digging of the ore was sub-contracted to Rowland Brotherhood of Chippenham, even so in the first year Sarl made over £5,000 profit.

In 1857 the Great Western Iron Ore, Smelting and Coal Co. Ltd., was established with the aim of smelting ore on the spot on the assumption that it would be more profitable to smelt the ore at Seend rather than to transport it to Staffordshire. It was proposed to set up four blast furnaces on about 6 hectares (15 acres) of land abutting the Kennet and Avon Canal and close to the Wilts, Somerset and Weymouth Railway, the throughput of which would be about 30,000 tonnes per annum selling at £5 a tonne. Money was swiftly invested, but the enterprise collapsed and the company went bankrupt in 1859.

Mr. Sarl had one of the furnaces completed which was put into blast in 1860, and a second in 1861, the two of which were producing 300 tonnes per week. The blast engine was a 120 h.p. beam and flywheel engine working at 14 lbs pressure, three boilers being used to generate steam. An article in the *Mining Journal* of May, 1861 attests to the quality of Wiltshire iron; however, by June, 1861 the company appears to have been in trouble again as the *Devizes Gazette* for June 6th, 1861 reports an attempt to raise capital to purchase the works.

This company, The Seend Iron Company Ltd., lasted just three years, being voluntarily wound up in March 1864; this was succeeded by the even more transient Wiltshire Iron Company with a life of 23 months almost to the day—22nd December, 1864 to 17th November, 1866.

From 1866 to 1870 the works were controlled by the landowners, Wadham Locke. In 1870 William and Samuel Malcolm of Glasgow were operating the furnaces, and in their turn went bankrupt in 1873. From 1873 to 1889 the works were operated by Richard Berridge, a partner in the London brewery of Sir Henry Meux. In 1889 the firm, finally beset by soaring freight charges and difficulties in maintaining markets, closed and the works were demolished and sold.

Although iron was no longer manufactured at Seend a further attempt was made in 1905 to extract the ore which was for several years sent to South Wales, and also used as a purifying agent in local gas works, but the venture came to an end and all production ceased.

At Westbury the deposits were first worked during the Roman period; more recently the extent of the deposit was noticed when a cutting was being made for the railway line in 1841. In 1857 the Westbury Iron Company was formed by a group of Radstock colliers.

Open cast mining techniques were used which have left their mark on the surrounding land, and two furnaces were erected north of the railway line, which were able to make about 250 tonnes of iron per week. In 1869 a second pair of furnaces was added, and by 1872 the works occupied about 4.8 hectares (12 acres), had about 1.6 km (1 mile) of tramways transporting ironstone and limestone, 12 calcinating kilns, 3 blast furnaces and hot air blast supplied by an 8 m (26 ft) beam engine with a 7.3 m (24 ft) flywheel fed by seven boilers. There were also three locomotives in the works.

The company appears to have been efficiently and profitably run until 1901 when increased costs and competition forced its closure. The works were offered to a group of local men, W. H. Laverton, J. Callaway and G. H. Knight and in 1903 restarted as the New Westbury Iron Company.

The new company struggled on till 1914 when the war requirements boosted producion to a total of 24,470 tonnes in 1917, but after the war the financial difficulties increased, and by 1925 all production had ceased. The works were finally auctioned off in 1939.

Gazetteer

Cotswold Limestone

1. Box Hill
2. Monk's Park, Corsham
3. Bradford-on-Avon
4. Leigh Delamere
5. Gastard

Corallian Stone

6. Workhouse Quarry, Calne

Portland Stone

7. Chilmark
8. Fonthill Lake
9. Chicksgrove
10. Tucking Mill Quarry, Tisbury
11. Teffont Evias

Swindon Stone

12. Okus Quarry
13. Town Garden

Chalk and Flint

14. Wanborough Church
15. Chitterne
16. Berwick St. James

Lime and Whiting

17. Kiln at East Knoyle
18. Kiln at Teffont Evias
19. West Harnham Quarry
20. Charnage Down Quarry
21. Quidhamptom Quarry

Sandstone

22. Sandy Lane
23. Potterne
24. Naish Hill Sandpit

Sarsen Stone

25. Avebury Village
26. Lockeridge Dene

Sand

27. Sahara Sand Pit
28. The Sands, Calne
29. High Penn Sand Pit

Clay

30. Caen Hill Brickworks
31. Badbury Brickworks
32. Purton Brickworks

Cement

33. Westbury Cement Works

Gravel

34. Ashton Keynes

Iron Workings

35. Seend
36. Westbury—Dilton Marsh

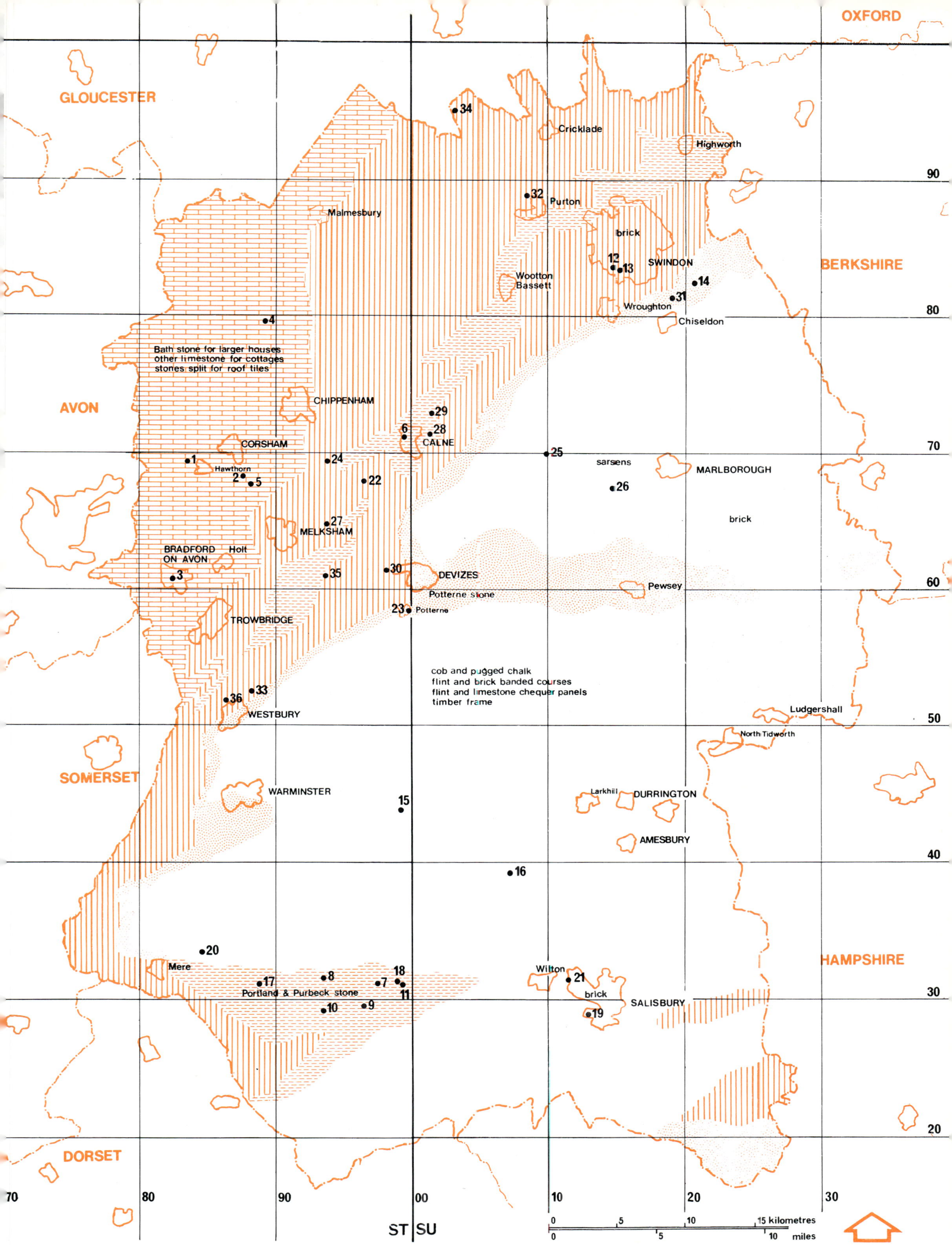

QUARRIES and sources of building materials

rock types : chalk, clay, gault clay & greensands, corallian, and oolite limestones

6. THE DEVELOPMENT OF AGRICULTURE

The earliest people to leave clear evidence of farming in Wiltshire were the Neolithic settlers, immigrants from Europe who began to come into southern England from about 3500 B.C. onwards, and who dominated the Wessex region until *c.* 2000 B.C., when they were in turn absorbed by a new wave of settlers from the Continent. The excavation of Neolithic sites in Wiltshire, most notably at Windmill Hill, near Avebury, but also at Knap Hill (Alton Barnes), Downton, Whitesheet Hill (Kilmington), Rybury (All Cannings), and elsewhere, has shown that, unlike their predecessors in the county, the Neolithic people depended upon agriculture for their livelihood, and that their farming included the breeding of cattle, including a long-horned type of ox, pigs, goats and sheep, and the growing of corn, particularly a form of wheat known as *emmer*. Few evidences remain in the Wiltshire landscape of their farming activities, and the most conspicuous survival of their occupation of the area consists of the long barrows in which they buried some of their dead, like the Neolithic long barrow at West Kennet near Avebury. From about 2000 B.C. the Bronze Age or 'Beaker' people began to arrive in Wiltshire from the Continent. Like their Neolithic predecessors, their farming included the breeding of cattle, sheep and pigs and the growing of corn, although at first barley rather than wheat was the main cereal crop. Later a new variety of wheat called *spelt* was introduced from the Continent. Again, few evidences survive in the landscape of the activities of the Bronze Age farmers, and their most prominent memorials consist of the very large number of round barrows in which they buried their dead.

Much more visible evidence survives of the activities of the Iron Age farmers since not only do their great hill forts continue to dominate many parts of the chalkland, but their 'Celtic' fields are still very clearly to be seen at many places on the chalk hillsides, for example at Bulford Down, Corton Down and most notably at Fyfield Down and Overton Down near Marlborough. These 'Celtic' fields are rectangular or square-shaped enclosures ranging from a quarter of an acre to two acres or more in size. The distinctive shape of the fields, which were used for growing crops, owes its origin to the type of shallow wooden plough drawn by small oxen, which was used by the Iron Age farmers. This was a primitive and inefficient instrument, which did little more than scratch a groove through the earth, and it was necessary to plough the land several times in both directions before a satisfactory tilth could be obtained; thus square or rectangular fields were the most suitable for such cultivation. This kind of farming continued throughout the Roman period, although a more advanced type of agriculture was practised on the estates associated with the Roman villas. The presence of the Roman armies increased the demand for corn, and much of it came from the chalklands of southern England including Wiltshire.

The Saxon invasion of Wiltshire following the withdrawal of the Romans from Britain in the 5th century A.D. led to a rapid extension of farming into the forests, which had previously covered much of the north and west Wiltshire, and into the clay vales. By the time of the Norman Conquest the pattern of settlement, the lay-out of manors and the siting of villages was already established over most of the county. Many of the villages which are in existence today were already strung out along the base of the chalk escarpments or along the river valleys of the chalkland; the high downland was devoted to sheep grazing, the arable lands occupied the lower slopes and the valley bottoms were reserved for the meadow land which produced the hay which was so essential if animals were to survive through the winter. By the time of the compilation of the Domesday Survey in 1086 the distinction was already well established between the chalk country, with its emphasis upon corn production and sheep farming, and the clay vales many of which were still heavily forested during the early Middle Ages, but where cattle rearing and dairy farming were already the main stays of agriculture. Sheep farming had expanded rapidly during the Saxon period, and very large flocks were kept on the chalklands throughout the Middle Ages. The sheep were valued for their wool, their mutton, their milk and also for their dung, since only by constant use of the sheep-fold could most of the thin chalkland soils be made to grow satisfactory crops of corn.

The population of Wiltshire increased rapidly during the 12th and 13th centuries, doubling in many places between 1086 and 1400, and this is reflected in the extension of the cultivated area on many manors, in the continued inroads which were made into the forests, marshes and waste grounds of the county and in the growth of new settlements, particularly on claylands. This period also saw the extension of cultivation up the steep hillsides of the chalkland by means of those strip lynchets or cultivation terraces which survive in many parts of the county and which enabled more land to be pressed into use.

By the 13th century, when a substantial amount of documentary evidence becomes available for the first time, sheep farming and the marketing of wool were already highly organised. Many manors had sheep flocks of more than 1000 animals and in many places even larger flocks were kept.

Much of the wool from Wiltshire sheep was exported in its raw state, but the local cloth industry developed rapidly in the later Middle Ages. By the 14th century Salisbury was one of the leading centres in the country both for the marketing of wool and the manufacture of cloth, and by the end of the 15th century there were also important centres of the cloth industry at Castle Combe, Bradford-on-Avon, Trowbridge, Steeple Ashton and Westbury. The white broadcloth of Wiltshire was famous in England and was in demand abroad.

Corn production was also important in the county throughout the Middle Ages, particularly on the chalklands. Here most manors had their arable lands in two or three large unenclosed fields and the strips of individual tenants were scattered throughout the fields. To preserve the fertility of the thin soils not only were they folded with the communal sheep flock, but one field was left fallow every year. Evidences of the existence of these former common arable fields can still be seen very clearly beneath later enclosures as at Steeple Ashton, Wedhampton, Longbridge Deverill and many other places, particularly in the chalklands. The crops most commonly grown were wheat as the main winter corn, together with oats and barley; peas and beans were sown in the spring.

The farming specialisation of the different regions of the county has continued to be a major feature of its agricultural development. From the early Middle Ages the clay vales of the north of the county, the 'cheese' country, were devoted to dairy farming and cattle raising. Here much of the pasture was enclosed during the Middle Ages, and in most places by the 16th century only rough grazing or marsh and woodland remained as open commons.

The central chalkland area was the sheep-corn region, where the vast sheep flocks kept by day on the downlands were folded at night on the arable land and their dung made it possible for large corn crops to be grown. This was the area in which the common arable fields survived longest and where the vast areas of common grazing on the downland remained unenclosed and used as sheep-pasture until the 19th century. In the north-west of the county at the southern extremity of the Cotswold Hills there was another region of sheep-corn husbandry where the shallow limestone soil demanded enrichment by the sheep-fold if it was to produce satisfactory corn crops. In the south of the county there were also pockets of heavier land which were devoted to dairy farming, cattle raising and the production of butter and cheese, and where there was very little arable farming. It is clear from many 17th century sources that the butter and cheese produced in the rich pastures of the north Wiltshire claylands was eagerly sought by merchants from London and other towns. John Aubrey, writing in the 1670s, praised the excellence of Wiltshire cheese and described Marlborough as "one of the greatest markets for cheese in the west of England. Here doe reside factors for the cheesemongers of London". Thirty years later, Defoe commented upon the amount of cheese which was produced in north Wiltshire and sent to London, Bath, Bristol and even exported to the West Indies. Defoe also noted another product which has continued to be very important in the economy of the county, and wrote "... the farmers in Wiltshire ... send a very great quantity of bacon up to London, which is esteemed as the best bacon in England, Hampshire only excepted: This bacon is raised in such quantities here, by reason of the great dairies, ... the hogs being fed with the vast quantity of whey, and skim'd milk, which so many farmers have to spare, and which must otherwise, be thrown away". In the chalk country sheep were vital for the maintenance of the fertility of the soil and it was for folding on the arable land that they were principally kept, their wool, lambs and mutton being an important but nonetheless secondary consideration for farmers.

The farming accounts which survive from the 17th century of Robert Wansborough who farmed on the chalkland at Shrewton, for example, show clearly that his principal profits came from corn and that his large sheep flock was valued principally as an essential element in the production of his grain crops. For a satisfactory sheep-fold it was necessary to have a very large number of sheep, so that they were kept in vast numbers on most chalkland manors, generally in a common flock under the supervision of a common shepherd. The Wiltshire Horn sheep were admirably suited for folding on arable land. They were large-limbed hardy animals, who could find their feed by day on the chalk downlands and could be driven down each evening to be close-folded on the lower-lying arable lands. They were slow to fatten and had only a light fleece, but they were excellent for folding, and their dung together with the consolidating action of their feet on the light chalkland soil, was the prime reason for the heavy yields of corn from this area.

The problem which had always limited the number of stock which could be kept, and thus restricted the amount of land which could be folded and dunged and the quantity of corn which could be grown, was that of providing sufficient feed during the winter, and particularly during the 'hungry' months of February, March and early April when the hay was exhausted and before the natural growth of grass occurred. This problem was partially overcome in the Wiltshire chalklands during the 17th century by the creation of water-meadows. The floated water-meadows were the greatest single development in agricultural technique between the Middle Ages and the farming development of the 19th century. The main purpose of the water-meadows was for encouraging a growth of grass much earlier than would have occurred naturally. This was achieved by constructing an elaborate network of channels and drains together with weirs and hatches so that water from a convenient stream was made to flow all over the surface of the meadow, thus covering the grass in a thin moving sheet of water, protecting it from frost and encouraging an early growth. To make a satisfactory water-meadow was a difficult and laborious business, since it was essential that it was so arranged that the water was kept moving over the surface, since stagnant water would kill the grass instead of encouraging its growth. The water-meadow grass provided early feed for sheep and lambs, at just the time when feed was scarce, and made it possible to keep larger flocks than would otherwise have been supported. This in turn greatly increased the folds and thus the corn-growing capacity of the chalklands. After the sheep had fed during March and April, the meadows could again be 'watered' and shut up for hay; and the water-meadows produced far larger crops of hay than unwatered meadows. The fast-flowing chalk streams of Wiltshire were ideal for watering meadows, since they could easily be diverted with hatches and made to overflow the meadows, and the water coming from the underground reservoirs of the chalk downland was comparatively warm and moreover contained a rich chalky sediment which was deposited amongst the stalks of the grass. The management of the meadows was a skilled business on chalkland manors and the 'floater' or 'drowner' was an important person in the manorial economy. The creation of water-meadows began in Wiltshire during the early 17th century, and the idea spread rapidly along the valleys of the chalk streams. By the early 19th century nearly 8,000 hectares (20,000 acres) of meadow land were being regularly watered in Wiltshire, and the water-meadows were an essential element in the farming of the chalkland region.

Until the 18th century most of the tools and implements used by Wiltshire farmers were of wood and were generally home-made. Few of these have survived, although collections of wooden implements and hand tools are to be seen at various places in the county, notably at the Wiltshire Agricultural College at Lackham and at Longhedge Farm, Corsley. Farmers' main implements included the plough or 'sull' which was generally made of ash, and was pulled by oxen or horses. Oxen were preferred by many farmers, particularly on heavier land, since, although they were slower than horses, they gave a stronger, steadier pull. Only with improvements in breeds of horses during the 19th century did the horse replace the ox as the main plough beast on many farms, and in some places oxen continued to be used into the 20th century.

Drags or harrows were commonly made of wood with iron tines; rollers were little used on the chalk where the feet of the folded sheep consolidated the newly cultivated land. The most expensive item of farmers' equipment was the wagon. These were little used before the later 17th century except by carriers, and John Aubrey wrote that the wagon was not introduced into south Wiltshire until after the Civil War. It was from the period of the Napoleonic Wars that the elaborately built farm wagon, the masterpiece of the wheelwright's and carpenter's art, really came into its own and the distinctive style of Wiltshire wagon was developed.

The farmers' hand tools included the hook, the scythe, the mattock, the spade and the axe. Wheat was cut with a 'bagging hook' which preserved the straw for thatching; hay and the other corn crops were cut with a scythe. Threshing with a flail and winnowing was a laborious process which occupied many men throughout the whole winter; threshed corn was stored in granaries, often built on 'staddle stones' to preserve it from rats and mice, and several examples of such granaries survive in the county.

During the later 17th century and throughout the 18th and 19th centuries, as well as watered meadows, a series of other innovations and improvements was adopted by Wiltshire farmers, being introduced at first on the large estates or by a few more progressive and go-ahead farmers, and gradually taken up by others. For example, the progress of enclosures continued particularly on the claylands; many drainage schemes were also introduced in these low-lying lands and many hundreds of acres reclaimed from marsh and bog, as well as from woodland and waste. New fertilizers were used such as marl and lime; new crops were slowly introduced—clover, rye-grass, sainfoin and other fodder crops, such as cabbages, rape, kale and turnips. The potato remained largely a garden crop until the early 19th century: thereafter it became an essential element in the diet of farm labourers and their families, without which many would have starved, particularly in the harsh years which followed the ending of the Napoleonic Wars in 1815. During the time of high corn prices caused by the Napoleonic Wars, however, the pace of progress and improvement accelerated. Large areas of the chalklands were enclosed by private Act of Parliament, and hedges transformed many previously open tracts of downland countryside.

The process of enclosure, while it undoubtedly resulted in a higher standard of farming, improved methods and increased yields, nonetheless often had disastrous effects for the small farmer who either could not afford the high cost of fencing or whose allotment of land in place of his former right of common grazing for his sheep and cattle was insufficient to support him and his family, and he was often compelled to sell his allotment of land and join the growing class of landless labourers. Enclosure therefore had the effect of increasing the size of farms and decreasing the number of farmers. Enclosure by Act of Parliament was a planned process, carried out by a surveyor working under Commissioners appointed by the Act. The results can be seen in parishes all over Wiltshire, for the Parliamentary surveyors laid out completely new landscapes with straight roads bounded by regular verges, geometrically planned fields of regular shape and size and generally also with similar hedges all composed of the same shrub species. Such areas can also be recognised by the fact that whereas previously all farmsteads had been clustered together in the villages, after enclosure new farms were often built out in the newly allotted and enclosed fields. These are often distinguishable by the fact that farm house and buildings are of one date often early 19th century, and commonly also by their names—e.g. New Zealand, Quebec, Newgrounds, New Leaze, Waterloo Barn (Ansty), Hougoumont Farm (Collingbourne Ducis).

During the early 19th century as a result of the changes and innovations which had been introduced, much of the farming of Wiltshire was of a very high standard. In 1822, for example, William Cobbett, who in his *Rural Rides*, had seen and critically examined the farming in many parts of England, could write of the Avon and Wylye valleys in south Wiltshire that he had seldom seen a finer countryside or land that was better farmed.

At Milton Lilborne he wrote "I never before saw anything to please me like this valley of the Avon. I sat upon my horse and looked over Milton, Easton and Pewsey for half an hour, though I had not breakfasted." and "It is impossible for the eyes of men to be fixed on a finer country than that between the village of Codford and the town of Warminster . . .". Cobbett went on to add that it was not easy to find anywhere else a labouring people who were more wretched; but this disagreeable fact did not blind him to the excellence of the agriculture which he saw in those chalkland valleys. Cobbett also commented favourably upon the farming which he saw in the northern part of the county, for example of the area between Wootton Bassett and Highworth he wrote, "This is a *cheese country*, some corn, but generally speaking, it is a country of dairies"; and of the area around Cricklade, "Here are some of the very finest pastures in all England, and some of the finest dairies of cows, from 40 to 60 in a dairy . . .".

The 19th century saw three developments of great importance in Wiltshire agriculture. The first was the introduction of new methods of stockbreeding and of new strains of sheep, cattle and pigs. Increasing population led to a greater demand for meat, and widespread attempts were made to increase the weight and mutton producing capacity of the Wiltshire Horn sheep by crosses with Southdowns and Leicesters, so that by the 1820s there were no pure Wiltshires left in the county. Later Hampshire and Dorset Down sheep were also introduced. The old mixed Longhorn and Gloucester cattle of north Wiltshire were also transformed by crosses and the introduction of new breeds such as Devonshires and Herefords and later by the Shorthorns. These were in turn ousted in favour of Ayrshires and later still by the now almost ubiquitous Friesians. Pig breeds were also changed out of all recognition during the 19th century, by the development of Large Whites, Large Blacks, Wessex Saddlebacks and other breeds. The second major development was in the facilities for transport; above all, the coming of the railways, which for the first time enabled farm produce to be carried quickly, easily and cheaply to London and other large centres of population. This led to a rapid decline in cheese making on farms within the county, to the virtual disappearance of the old cheeses, such as the Gloucester and Wiltshire loaf cheeses, and to the growth of cheese factories, most of them producing a standardised Cheddar type cheese. New transport facilities also led to the substitution of the export of liquid milk for the old trade in farm-produced butter and cheese, and to the establishment within the county of factories for milk processing and for the wholesale production and distribution of condensed milk, butter and cream, as well as cheese and other dairy products.

The third main development of the 19th century was the introduction of mechanisation to farming and the application of steam power. From the 18th century onwards there were steady improvements in implements, the introduction of drills, lighter iron harrows, wheeled iron ploughs, deep drainage ploughs, and, later, threshing machines and elevators. These innovations produced several Wiltshire inventors, developers and manufacturers of farm implements, including Moses Boorn of Barford near Downton who invented a corn drill in 1789, J. Trowbridge of Amesbury who invented a winnowing machine, and J. Fowler who was born at Melksham in 1826 and who experimented with both drainage and steam ploughs. Several major firms of agricultural engineers were founded in Wiltshire during the 19th century. T. P. Reeves of Bratton who died in 1848 began the manufacture of a range of agricultural implements at Bratton during the early 19th century, including ploughs, drills, rollers, harrows and all sorts of other farming equipment. The firm of Brown and May of Devizes carried on a very large business during the 19th century, producing among other things engines for steam ploughing. Stationary steam engines were used first for milling and barn work, later travelling engines were extensively used to drive threshing machines, and in the late 19th century were also used for steam ploughing. Thomas Pope of Ogbourne St. George started an agricultural engineering business in the mid 19th century, and the firm moved to Marlborough in 1870. Hugh Carson of Warminster set up a foundry there in 1816 producing agricultural implements, and there were a great many other small firms set up all over the county during the 19th century, for supplying implements to farmers.

The dramatic upheavals which have occurred in the fortunes of agriculture since the later 19th century and the effects of these changes are well-known and can be dealt with very briefly here. The use of machinery has increased tremendously and the tractor has replaced the horse. The labour force has dwindled from 27,000 farm workers in the county in 1871 to 4,520 in 1971, while even more dramatically the female labour force on farms has dropped from 5,000 in 1871 to 840 in 1971.

Farms have tended to get larger, particularly on the chalklands where much of the old downland grazing has succumbed to the plough and is now used as permanent arable. With the vastly increased use of artificial fertilizers the old role of the sheep as a 'walking dung-cart' vanished, and the number of sheep kept in the county dropped from 774,000 in 1870 to 73,000 in 1954. Apart from a few survivals, water-meadows have almost entirely gone out of use; improved strains of grasses, new fertilizers, the heavy labour costs involved in their upkeep, and, above all, the difficulty of using tractors and heavy machinery on the soft ground of the meadows without damaging the intricate net-work of channels and drains, have all been factors in their decline.

Dairy herds have increased greatly in average size with the disappearance of many of the smaller dairy and mixed farms. One important development in dairy farming between the wars originated in the county; this was the Hosier bail milking system, an easily transportable milking parlour which was used in the fields and which meant that lands remote from the farmstead could nonetheless support herds of dairy cows. The system was invented between the wars by A. J. Hosier of Wexcombe and rapidly became popular in many parts of the country. In the Wiltshire dairy herds the Friesian has ousted most of the older breeds of milking cows, and 'Cheddar' cheese has driven the native varieties out of existence.

Above all, the modern use of imported feedstuffs and silage for cattle, modern methods of powered cultivation and harvesting, the intensive application of artificial fertilizers, modern methods of weed and pest control and new developments in stock breeding and management, have all vastly increased the agricultural output of the county as well as totally altering the appearance of the farms and of the countryside.

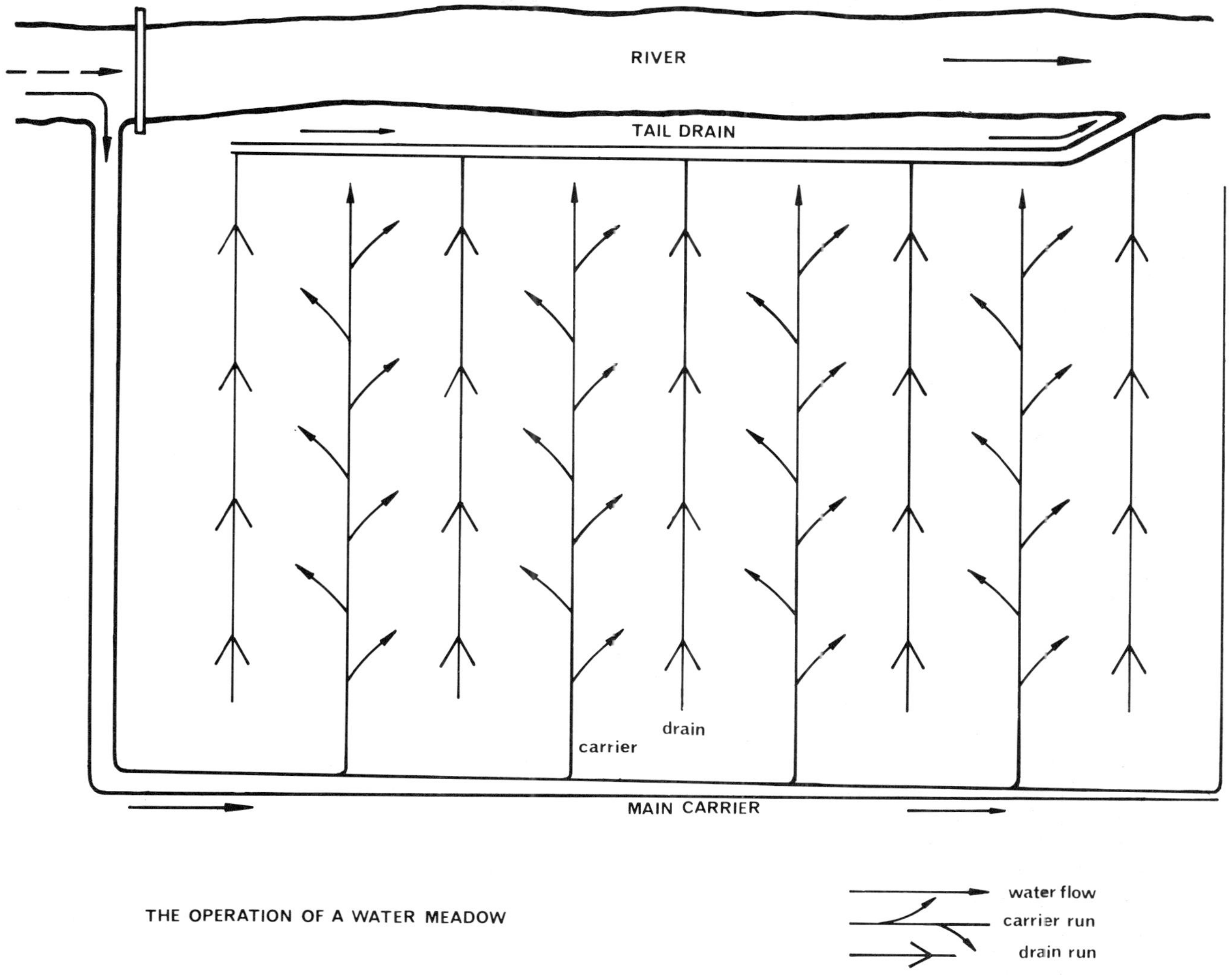

THE OPERATION OF A WATER MEADOW

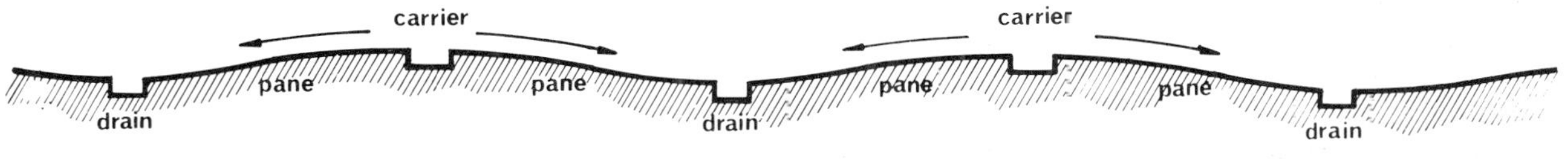

part CROSS-SECTION

WATER MEADOWS: the principle of operation

***Longford*: *Watermeadows beside the River Avon.* (*Photo., Devizes Museum*)**

Oxplough team on the downs at Aldbourne.
(*Photo., Devizes Museum*)

Wiltshire Horn ram. (*Photo., Devizes Museum*)

North Wiltshire wagon. (*Photo., Museum of English Rural Life*)

7. SOME OTHER INDUSTRIES

Engineering

The end of the 18th century and the beginning of the 19th saw the emergence of the profession of the engineer. There had doubtless been a long tradition of men skilled in the rudiments of engineering who had been responsible for the building and maintenance of the wind, water and animal mills with which the county abounded. It was natural that from this reservoir of expertise, and from the blacksmiths and carpenters of the villages, that many of those who were to become the engineers should arise. It was the mechanisation of the textile industry which gave rise to the specialist millwrights, whose task it was to build and assemble the machinery used in the manufacture of cloth; the mechanisation of agricultural practices resulted in the founding of a large number of firms specialising in this type of work; improvements in transportation gave rise to civil and mechanical engineers. The provision of public utilities brought a new group of engineers skilled in the manufacture and installation of gas fittings, lighting, heating and plumbing. Finally, changes in the urban situation led to many industries seeking advantages away from the traditional centres of industry, such advantages were found for many in Wiltshire.

Specialist millwrighting was, like the textile industry, centred on Trowbridge and Bradford-on-Avon. In Bradford, Job Wastfield and Samuel Godwin are the first of these engineers to be specifically described as millwrights in a trade directory (1816); there are earlier references, for example John Ebsworth of Cricklade St. Samson in his will of 1614 is described as a millwright. In 1815 George Haden had been sent to Trowbridge and had installed himself as agent for the famous Birmingham steam engine firm of Boulton & Watt. Boulton & Watt had in fact converted the first factory to steam power, that of John Cooper in Duke Street, Trowbridge in 1805, and prior to that, there had been mills powered by animal and water sources of some sophistication. It is obvious therefore that skilled engineers were working in the county well before those first recorded in trade directories.

It was in Trowbridge, with George Haden that the principal firm in the trade was established. Haden had been apprenticed to Boulton & Watt by his father, who worked at the Soho manufactory in the shop making an early form of copying machine invented by Watt. As an experienced engineer, George had been entrusted with the installation of engines in the Manchester and Glasgow cotton factories; however, he was not enamoured by these towns, and when sent to Trowbridge to install an engine for J. & T. Clarke found the town much more to his liking. Dissatisfied with his terms of employment with Boulton & Watt, he requested an agency to sell their engines in Wiltshire, Somerset and Gloucestershire which was granted. The work from steam engines was insufficient and Haden sought permission to undertake millwork on his own account. Joined by now by his brother James, the orders grew, and as the small upper floor workshop was found inadequate, a factory was acquired in Silver Street. Numerous patents were taken out by the Hadens for new machinery for dressing cloth; not all were related to the use of steam power, plans of 1883 were for water-powered equipment.

It was in the field of heating, particularly of large public buildings that the main work of the firm was to lie. George Haden took out patents for several types of warm air stove, and installed plant in many ecclesiastical, public and private buildings and institutions including Westminster Abbey, the British Museum, and nearer home, Longleat and Wilton House. Arising from this work the firm started to provide not only heating but institutional kitchens and other related services. George's son, George Nelson Haden, developed new forms of hard labour devices which were quickly adopted in most prisons in the country, one a crank which had to be turned a specified number of times before meals were served; the other, an improved treadmill, was used to work machinery, or, failing this was governed by a wind fan, apparatus known by the Trowbridge workers as a 'wind grinder'.

The work soon exceeded the capacity of the Silver Street works and Haden went into partnership with Woodfin in 1825 in the St. George's Foundry on the corner of Stallard Street and the present Bythesea Road. St. George's works became a major factor in the company and was in use until 1910 when it was closed. In 1913 the works were taken over by the Wilts United Dairy as its headquarters. This firm, now Unigate, still occupies the site, which is substantially unchanged.

In 1947 Haden's decided to cease production and concentrate on installation of plant. They left Trowbridge, and their Silver Street works were taken over by Newman Hender, later Hattersley, Newman Hender Ltd. Subsequently this firm moved to works in Bradley Road which had been occupied by Vickers Armstrong.

Most other engineering firms in Trowbridge were associated with Haden's. In 1907 Roberts, a pattern maker who had been a foreman at St. George's Foundry, went into partnership with Arthur Morris, a former apprentice with Isaac Cordingly (see below) and also an employee of Haden's. Roberts & Morris' foundry, first in Innox Lane and later in Shails Lane made some of the castings required by Haden's, and also for the Gauntlet Carding Machine Company. This latter company had been founded in Union Street in 1878, and later, in 1920 moved to Shails Lane where it remained until 1949; most of their output went to the upholstery trade and to poor law institutions by whom it was used to open out flock, but machinery was also exported, particularly to Australia. In 1949 the work was taken over by Roberts and Morris.

Isaac Cordingly was also based in Innox Lane. This was a short lived firm founded by an employee of Spencers of Melksham (see below) which seems to have failed due to Cordingly turning his attention to gas engines.

In 1833 a Trowbridge engineer, John Dyer, patented a machine for fulling to replace the mill stocks; although he sold the patent he retained the right to produce the machine himself as many used in Trowbridge were supplied by him.

In Bradford the same diversification seems to have occurred, first into agricultural engineering; and later, with the arrival in Bradford of the rubber industry, into the production of castings of moulds and the maintenance of machinery for rubber manufacture. In 1830 Charles Milsom had works "Near the bridge"; he was described as a millwright and engineer, his brother George as an iron and brass founder and agricultural machinist. In 1914 the Milsoms handed over to Berkely Uncles, a former apprentice, who went into partnership with W. T. Jackson. It was these two who were to be principally involved in serving the rubber works. Later, the firm of S. J. Brierley (Wilts) Ltd., operating from Trowbridge Road also specialised in this work as did the Altus Engineering Co. of Stokes Road, Corsham, who commenced operations in 1935, and later also supplied moulds to the plastics industry.

In Melksham, W. Eyres was described as brightsmith, millwright, mechanical engineer and iron founder in 1830; his works were probably those occupied by John Gillett at the corner of Union and Bank Street in 1872. In 1878 Gillett was joined by C. J. Spencer and the firm became Spencers of Melksham. In the 1880s W. Littlejohn Phillip became manager of the firm and later chairman. Phillip concentrated on the manufacture of bulk grain handling equipment. His first major contract was for the Humber Elevator Co. of Hull, and soon after Spencers were supplying equipment for every port in the country, and many abroad. In 1905 large floating cranes were supplied to the Port of London. In 1903 the firm moved into new works in Beanacre Road. These works were taken over with the firm in 1966 by Elliot Automation which in turn was acquired by English Electric, subsequently the General Electric Company. Two firms of civil engineers were active in Melksham in 1847. J. Pritchard of Colony Place, Melksham was described as a railway contractor, while in 1900 Tilke and Smith were road plant contractors who later installed electric light in the district.

In Calne the leading engineering firm was that founded by Edward Ward Maundrell in a disused chapel in London Road. In 1885 he went into partnership with Ernle Woodward who had worked with John Fowler, the Leeds portable engine maker, born in Melksham in 1826. Woodward was thus conversant with the techniques of steam ploughing. Soon after Maundrell and Woodward separated and Woodward set up as a steam plough proprietor and engineer. From a small beginning making penny-farthing bicycles, Maundrell's progressed to the manufacture of agricultural machinery, and castings required locally. It was the mechanisation of the factory of C. & T. Harris which brought the business to prominence and having made and installed the machinery, they were approached by other firms in the trade, not only in this country, but also in Ireland, Denmark, South Africa and New Zealand.

Early engineering in Chippenham was closely associated with the railway. In 1848 Rowland Brotherhood started up the Railway Works at New Road. Brotherhood had been one of the principal contractors on the building of the railway in Wiltshire, and was associated with Brunel, the railway engineer. At his works at Chippenham and at Swindon, Brotherhood built locomotives which were exported to many parts of the world. They also built carriages for the Great Western Railway. The building of the Swindon Railway Works led to a decline in the work of the firm which closed by the 1890s. In 1870 the G.W.R. rented carriage works at Chippenham described as "lately belonging to Mr. Brotherhood".

In 1880 G. Hathaway bought land in New Road from Brotherhood where he made dairy equipment, and in 1885 T. Hathaway was in the same business in St. Paul's Road. In 1903 the site of Brotherhood's works, and a foundry of H. G. Phipps was occupied by Evans and O'Donnell, a leading firm in the manufacture of railway signal equipment. Later this firm and others in the signal trade became the Consolidated Signal Co. In 1920 the company was acquired by the Westinghouse Brake Company, later the Westinghouse Brake and Signal Company, still the leading firm in the area and the principal firm in railway signalling and brake manufacture in the country.

Swindon, prior to the building of the railway, was a market town of little industrial consequence, overshadowed by neighbours such as Highworth. The brass and iron foundry of George Kerr in Victoria and Albert Street occasionally made steam engines; founded in 1852 the firm was taken over in 1856 by W. V. Edwards, an ironmonger. Under Edwards, castings were made for the domestic trade, principally gas fittings, and the gas companies' equipment was maintained. In 1861 the firm was known as Edwards and Suter, and the works, Castle Foundry. Agricultural implements and dairy utensils were made as well as items for the continuing and flourishing ironmongery trade.

The proximity of the railway was one of the stimuli for the growth of Swindon as an engineering centre. Among the early arrivals was Garrard and Company. In 1915 Garrard, the Crown jewellers, seeing the need to diversify and wishing to contribute to the war effort, set up a subsidiary, the Garrard Engineering and Manufacturing Co. In 1919 this subsidiary was moved to Newcastle Street in Swindon. Established as a precision engineering company, at the end of the war the firm decided to concentrate on the production of gramophone motors, and later clocks and automatic record changers.

Devizes was the centre for the manufacture of mobile steam engines. In 1842 William Box was described as an engineer at Bath Road, Devizes, and subsequently at Northgate Street, the Nursery and at Poulshot in 1847, 1848 and 1855 respectively. In 1850 he was described as a steam engine maker at Market Lavington. His firm was acquired by T. H. White.

One of the leading firms in Devizes during the second half of the 19th century, and a leading firm in the country in the field of steam transportation, was Brown and May. In 1854 William Brown and Charles May opened an engineering works at Estcourt Street to manufacture agricultural equipment and portable (mobile) steam engines. May had been connected with the Ipswich firm of Ransomes and May. The firm played a significant role in the development of the steam engine; boilers with very long fireboxes were made for burning wood and straw, fuels found in underdeveloped countries, and locomotive-type boilers were designed which could be used in confined spaces enabling steam engines to be installed in cargo carrying lorries. At the turn of the century a track laying vehicle was developed which was well ahead of its time; economies of fuel were effected by the use of exhaust heat to preheat water. It was probably the versatility of the firm's engineers that led to the early success of the company, agents were appointed in this country and in various parts of the world—three were in Russia.

The successors to the founders attempted to expand into the manufacture of oil engines but were unable to compete with the leaders in the field, and despite continuing sales of steam engines, the firm was wound up in 1913. The works are now occupied by the civil engineering firm of W. E. Chivers. One other person, J. Clissold, is mentioned in 1868 as making portable steam engines at the Phoenix Foundry, also in Devizes.

T. H. White is one of the leading firms of agricultural engineers in central Wiltshire. Founded in the middle of the last century by George White it grew by the acquisition of several smaller firms; T. Pope Ltd. of the High Street, Marlborough, and formerly of Ogbourne St. George was acquired at an early date; William Box, mentioned above, was acquired about 1890 and H. G. Phipps, an iron founder and engineer of Chippenham about 1914.

Agricultural engineering was also practised in Warminster; Hugh Carson established his foundry in 1816 and in 1847 is specifically mentioned as an agricultural implement maker. He operated from East Street and the Portway. Various machines and pieces of equipment were produced, a sophisticated chaff-cutter, an automatic sheep creep among others. In 1906 the founder's grandson emigrated to Canada, selling the firm. John Wallis Titt was sent to Warminster by Brown and May in 1870, as their agent. Four years later he had set up on his own as representative of a number of firms, and in the following year he opened a factory at Woodcock, near the railway. At the turn of the century he was still an agent, made wire fencing and an advanced design of elevator, but his main work was in water supply. He specialised in boring artesian wells, supplying pipework and pumps, but principally in wind pumps (see page 29). Contracts were obtained, not only in England, but also in Italy and West Africa.

The leading firm of agricultural engineers was undoubtedly that founded by Thomas Pepler Reeves at Bratton in 1808. During the first quarter of the 19th century he was joined in business by his sons, and by 1859 they were renowned as makers of ploughs and seed drills. During the latter half of the century the range of implements manufactured increased; the firm also acted as agent for others in the same trade, such as Brown and May and Hathaways of Chippenham.

In the south of the county Salisbury was the centre of engineering activity. Chiefly worthy of note is the Scout Motor Car Co., the only motor car firm in Wiltshire. In 1888 a clock making business was founded by the father of Albert and William Burden at 101 Fisherton Street, with works at Wilton Road, on the site of Moody's Depository. In 1901 these works were sold to Williamson and Sons of London who ran them as the English Clock Factory. New premises were acquired, the Excelsior Works in Friary, in which the brothers made motor boats and motor cycles. In the same year Percy Dean of Chitterne became a director and injected capital of £3,800. The following year the style of the firm was changed from Dean & Burden Bros. to the Scout Motor Co., and a year later in 1905, the first Scout Motor car appeared. Scouts had had many successes in regattas with their motor boats, and in 1906 the Motor Yacht Club awarded the Scout River Boat their Certificate of Reliability. In the same year the Automobile Club of Great Britain awarded a medal to a Scout car which came ninth out of a field of 26 in the Isle of Man Tourist Race. Success of the firm and a demand for its products led to a demand for new factory space; in 1906 this was built in Bemerton Road, Churchfields, now the site of a Post Office communications depot. The works comprised two foundries, a pattern shop, forges and an erecting bay. Four standard models were produced, and by 1909 a further two models were added to the range. 1909 was also a notable year in that it saw the end of production of motor boats and the commencement of manufacture of commercial vehicles, delivery vans of 10 cwt., 15 cwt. and 20 cwt. capacity.

1912 was the peak of production with two vehicles a week being finished, but the small output was even then being threatened by high output American factories. It was also in 1912 that the first bus was produced for Hall and Co. of Orcheston, to be followed by numerous others for carriers in the villages around Salisbury. In 1915 the Wilts and Dorset Motor Services were formed in Amesbury and of their first seven buses six were Scouts. The buses were particularly suited to the narrow country roads for which they were made.

At the beginning of the First World War there was little change in the output of the company although their products were used by the military and the police; however, in 1915 the factory machinery was removed to France where it was used to service vehicles close to the front. The firm was directed to produce bombs and mine mechanisms.

It was not until 1920 that motor production was resumed after protracted arguments over war compensation. However, competition was acute, Morris had set up his Cowley works, Fords had a mass production line, and despite the excellence of their vehicles the firm was wound up in 1921. The basic fault of the company would appear to be that too many models were produced, and that every part was made in Salisbury, thus output and profits were too low to compete with the market.

Food Processing

In two areas of food processing Wiltshire excelled, and was nationally renowned for its products; these were interrelated. Up to the 19th century large quantities of cheese were made, as well as the butter which may

Advertisement in the Wiltshire & Devizes Gazette of 1854

NORTH WILTS FOUNDRY, DEVIZES.

BROWN AND MAY,

ENGINEERS, IRON & BRASS FOUNDERS, BOILER MAKERS, AND GENERAL MACHINISTS,

BEG to inform their friends and agriculturists generally, that they are now in a position to execute all orders in the several branches of their business with punctuality and dispatch.

B. & M will be happy to supply Fixed or Portable Steam Engines, Thrashing and Winnowing Machines, Drills, Ploughs, Harrows, Scarifiers, Horse Hoes and Rakes, Rollers, Clod-crushers, Waggons, Carts, Chaff and Trnip Cutters, Cake-breakers, Grinding and Crushing Mills, and every other description of Farm Machinery, on the latest improved principles.

All kinds of Engineering and Mill Work executed.

IRON AND BRASS CASTINGS.

Also Park Fencing, Palisading, Tomb Railings, &c.

B. & M., in soliciting orders assure those who may favor them with their patronage, that every exertion shall be used on their part to insure their future support and recommendation, both as regards the economy of their charges and the superior quality of their materials and workmanship.

N.B.—Agents to all the principal Makers.

An Illustrated Price List sent free on application.

Threshing using an 8 NHP Brown & May steam engine
(*Photo., Devizes Museum*)

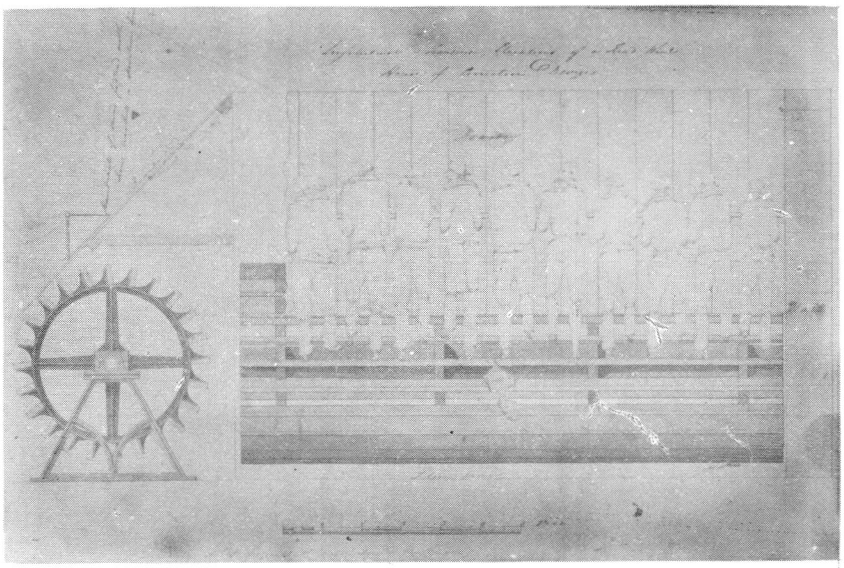

Treadwheel made by G. & N. Haden of Trowbridge for the Devizes House of Correction. Similar wheels were made by Haden's for most prisons in the country (from the original in Wilts. Record Office)

have been expected in an agricultural area, and by the 19th century Wiltshire bacon was a well-known product. The area of activity was predominantly the north and west of the county, pigs were fattened on the whey, a by-product of cheese manufacture.

The industrialization of bacon manufacture in Wiltshire was due to the expansion of the firm of C. and T. Harris of Calne. In the late 18th century John Harris opened a small butcher's shop in Calne which stood on the drove road for Irish pigs travelling from Bristol to London. It was these pigs which became the principal source for Harris' sons who had opened shops of their own in which they cured their own bacon. The Irish potato famine of 1847 brought a shortage of pigs, and to overcome this George Harris went to America to explore the possibility of shipping cured pigs to England. He visited many curers, and opened a curing house in Shenectady. This failed, and George returned to Calne. With him he brought the technique of using ice to cool the bacon in hot weather and by the use of ice-houses the firm was able to cure throughout the year and replace the hard salted cure with milder treatments. These techniques gave Harris an unrivalled lead over other English bacon curers. Income from the use of the ice-house patent by most other English bacon curers allowed Harris to mechanise the works. In the present century the firm was expanded into the manufacture of subsidiary products such as meat pies, and its factory is now a dominant feature of the town.

In Trowbridge one Abraham Bowyer began curing bacon in a grocer's shop in Fore Street in the early 19th century; by 1880, the business was in the hands of Abraham's son Elijah, production had expanded, and the Innox Mill had been acquired; the firm was described as "Wholesale bacon curers, cheese factors, millers and grocers". In the late 19th century the firm became a public company, and by 1924 control was acquired by the Harris family who had ceased to control the Calne firm in 1920. From that time the firm has expanded to occupy other former mill buildings in Trowbridge.

There were many other small bacon processing firms which did not achieve national importance and failed to survive to the present day. They are significant in that they have left a legacy of buildings typical of the industry. Most are situated in the north and west of the county. In Malmesbury, Adye and Hinwood had a capacity of 200 pigs a week at their factory, and at Warminster, Frank Moody Ltd., 250 pigs at Fore Street. In Chippenham the Wiltshire Bacon Curing Co. Ltd., manufactured Royal Wilts Bacon and Bradenham Ham as well as other pig products; in 1902 the firm was taken over by C. & T. Harris who operated it as a subsidiary. The Central Wiltshire Bacon Co. Ltd. at Bath Road, Devizes was formed in 1899, and survived until 1959 when the factory had a capacity of 350 pigs a week. The works, little altered, are now occupied by Cross Engineering Ltd.

The only factory of any consequence in the south of the county was the South Wilts Bacon Curing Co. at Downton, founded in 1929 in the former Workhouse and Prison; the directors were local meat merchants and farmers each seeking to provide the local retail trade with meat. In 1934 the company was taken over by I. Beer & Sons Ltd. of London, a take-over which gave the firm the capital to participate in the Bacon Development Scheme of the Ministry of Agriculture and through that scheme to expand, until after the war the company had a capacity of 1,600 pigs a week.

Dairy production, like the bacon industry, was to become concentrated in the hands of two main producers. Up to the 19th century surplus milk had been made into cheese for which Wiltshire was famed. Two factors changed the situation, firstly a cattle plague in London in 1868, and secondly the manufacture of sweetened, condensed milk.

In 1873 the Anglo-Swiss Condensed Milk Co., later the Nestlé Co. Ltd., opened the first milk factory in Wiltshire in a former mill at Bath Road, Chippenham; in 1897 a second was opened at the former mill at Staverton, and in 1914 a third at Fisherton Anger, Salisbury. The main work of the factories was and still is the production of condensed and evaporated milk.

In 1886 the Anglo Swiss Company did not renew the contracts of a number of farmers in Melksham, and the farmers persuaded Charles Maggs to establish a small factory in Staverton Road, Melksham. Maggs sold the separated milk back to the farmers as feed. In 1888 the dairy moved to New Broughton Road.

In 1889 the North Wiltshire Dairy Co. was formed by Reginald Butler. A factory was built at Pans Lane, Devizes, from which the main product was butter; in 1896 the company initiated the manufacture of Bondon and soft curd cheese. In 1897 Maggs Dairy and the North Wilts Dairy Co. combined to form the Wilts United Dairies, and were joined by several other dairies. Milk products were the chief output of the new company, but in 1901 a wholesale milk firm was acquired in Paddington, and the supply of milk to London became an increasing part of the business. In 1913 the company's offices were moved from Pans Lane in Devizes to the former Haden's Foundry in Bythesea Road, Trowbridge, which is still the head office of their successor, the Unigate Company.

In 1920 Wilts United Dairies acquired the Salisbury, Semley and Gillingham Dairy Co. Established at Semley in 1871 this company is renowned as the earliest wholesale milk firm in Wiltshire. One other firm to be drawn in to the United Dairy organisation was Aplin and Barrett who had a factory at Westbury at which cheddar cheese from other factories at Yeovil and Frome was made into processed cheese.

India Rubber

In 1848 Stephen Moulton, who has been associated with the American rubber pioneers, returned to England, and was attracted to Bradford-on-Avon by several factors—availability of suitable buildings in the shape of Kingston Mill, vacant since 1842, availability of cheap power and washing water in the River Avon, proximity to Bristol with good communications with London and last but not least a local benefactor, Captain Septimus Palairet who put up £5,000 for a share of Moulton's American associates with whom Moulton had a co-partnership agreement. In 1891

Moultons were joined by George Spencer and Co. and further premises were acquired, Church Street Mill and Abbey Mill in 1926.

In 1874 Giles and Willie Holbrow purchased the former cloth mill at Limpley Stoke and converted it to the manufacture of rubber; in 1886 Giles Holbrow retired and the mill and equipment were leased to Browne and Margetson; Willie Holbrow remained as manager. Railway springs were the main output of the factory, and as output expanded the Limpley Stoke factory was found to be inadequate and so in 1889 the works were moved to another woollen mill in Melksham. At the same time the partnership was converted to a public company, the Avon India Rubber Co. Ltd.

In the present century the emphasis has shifted from rubber components for railways to pneumatic tyres for motor cars, and with this shift there has been a dramatic expansion of the company and of its works at Melksham. In 1956 the company purchased George Spencer, Moulton and Co. Ltd., which it continues to operate and develop.

Brewing

Up to the end of the 19th century brewing was in the main undertaken by the landlords of the inns. Outside the Artichoke public house in Northgate Street, Devizes, a light advertises the Artichoke Brewery; the Bell Inn at Seend is a good example of a rural brew-house commonly used until the establishment of the large brewing companies.

An examination of the directories for Wiltshire shows the change from small scale brewing dramatically. In 1867 there were 95 brewers and 121 maltsters; in 1903 the brewers were reduced to 65 and the maltsters to 36, by this time the four firms which were to dominate the industry in later years were included—Ushers of Trowbridge, Wadworths of Devizes, Gibbs Mew of Salisbury, and Arkells of Swindon.

Closely allied to brewing, malting establishments can be recognised by their familiar vented conical or pyramidal roofs, and survive in many places. Major maltings are to be found in Warminster, which was renowned for its product which was distributed over the West of England; in 1818 the town had 25 malt-houses, the only surviving one was built in Pound Street in 1879. The malthouse in Leigh Road, Westbury is a fine example. In New Park Street, Devizes the facade of number 44 conceals a small malting complex of malting shed, bar and a bottle shaped kiln unique to the county and possibly dating from the 17th century.

The surviving breweries, both those still in use and those no longer used, present a range of styles. Arkells Brewery at Stratton St. Margaret in a compact group with a sign proclaining itself the Kingsdown Steam Brewery and dated 1861, is the oldest working brewery in the county; at Salisbury the Gibbs Mew Brewery in Gigant Street is a good example of a late 19th century brewery; the brewery at Trowbridge, now operated by Watney Mann (West) Ltd., and formerly the Ushers Brewery, has a fine brick facade to Back Street; Seven Stars Brewery, Wine Street, Bradford-on-Avon, now no longer operating, is a massive stone-built structure of about 1840, the main block of five stories carried on large arches, and the whole structure has the durable looking appearance of a fortress.

An examination of the history of the Wadworth Brewery at Devizes shows how the industry became concentrated in the hands of the few surviving companies. In 1768 Rose and Tylee were brewing in the former silk mill of Anstie; in 1875 the brewery was purchased by Henry Wadworth, and in 1885 moved to the present site which had been designed and built by Wadworth; in 1889 the Southbroom Brewery was purchased, followed in 1896 by the Bromham Brewery and in 1903 by the Estcourt Brewery; in 1904, the maltings in Northgate Street, Devizes were purchased, and finally, expanding beyond Wiltshire, Garne and Sons Brewery at Burford was acquired. From 1904 many licensed houses and hotels were bought, which doubtless included those such as the Artichoke (see above) in which brewing had been practised. Until 1976 the brewing operation was carried out using the original 1885 equipment and to the present day the method of brewing is identical to that carried out at the turn of the century.

Leather

Tanning has been carried out from an early date. Tanner was a common Wiltshire surname, and it is known that there was a tannery at Malmesbury in the early 13th century, at Devizes in 1371 and at Wilton in 1383; similar references can be found for most of the towns of the county at this time. In the 15th century there were guilds in Salisbury for tanners, skinners, curriers and shoemakers, saddlers and dubbers who included bookbinders, parchment makers and glovers. It is probable that the intensity of activity was linked to the woollen industry and sheep rearing. J. & T. Beaven of Holt, who are the oldest tanning firm still in existence, combined tanning with woolstapling and fellmongering up to 1937. The chief requirements of a tannery were an abundant supply of running water and a good source of oak bark. In both respects Wiltshire was well suited to the industry.

The 19th century saw, as in other industries, a change from the individual leather worker to a factory system, though the records of J. & T. Beaven go back to 1783, and the firm claims origins back to the 17th century. This firm concentrated on the manufacture of leggings and gloves in the latter part of the 19th century and the crust oil method was introduced at this time, but oak bark tanning was used up to 1920. The factory at Holt comprises brick built offices converted from cottages acquired in 1758 and a three-storey factory building surmounted by a bell turret and clock.

Case and Sons started tanning in 1900 at the former Boyers Mill, Westbury Leigh. The firm became specialists in the chrome tanning of kid skins imported from the Far East and Africa. Since the Second World War, buckskins and calf leathers have been introduced but kid remains the main product.

In 1930 the Downton Tanning Co. took over a tannery which had been founded and built in 1919 by the Southern Tanning Co. Sole leathers from oxhide are produced for the shoe manufacturers. This tannery is partially operated by water and has an interesting wheel (see above page 32).

J. & T. A. Smith of Lacock and Chippenham specialised in the production of oak bark tanned leather until it closed in 1928. The tannery still survives at Lacock.

Ware Bros. of Salisbury occupied the site of the Invicta Leather Works in Endless Street, founded in 1824. In 1901 the factory was destroyed by fire, and a new one built at Paynes Hill, which is now demolished. In 1936 the firm was taken over by a group of Germans who wished to specialise in the tanning of reptile skins. The activity continues to the present elsewhere in the city.

Closely allied to leather production, and surviving to the present, the gloving industry probably developed in the 19th century due to the decline in domestic dairying and textile industries releasing female labour which could be used as outworkers. The firm of J. & T. Beaven mentioned above was one of the first to estanlish a gloving fctory; this was in the former Spa Hotel, in which the cutting was done, the sewing being done by outworkers, some as far afield as the Cotswolds.

William Boulton of the firm of Boulton Bros. Ltd. of Westbury Leigh, and now of Warminster is renowned in glove manufacture as the inventor of the Boulton Cut Thumb, a method of cutting the thumb in gloves. Founded in 1871, the firm specialised in the making of quality and specialist gloves. A number of factories were used, the original being Indigo Factory in Eden Vale, a former dye factory. In 1901 a grist mill was bought and a new factory built adjacent, and in 1932 another company was founded at Westbury by V. C. Boulton. There was also a small workshop in Devizes.

Also in Westbury, the Jefferies were high quality glove makers. A firm was set up in Fore Street in 1883 by A. L. & W. L. Jefferies who had been apprenticed to the cloth trade, and made gloves as a hobby. The success of the firm led to the addition of tanning and leather dressing in 1889, and a mill was acquired for this at Hawkeridge in 1908. In the 1920s the firm expanded rapidly, branches were opened at Warminster, where a factory was started in Station Road, and beyond the county in Frome, Misdomer Norton, Radstock and Southampton. In 1936 the firm was taken over by Dent, Allcroft and Co. Ltd. of Worcester and London; however a new firm was set up in Gillingham by George Jefferies with branches in Westbury and Warminster. The firm is now based in Westbury.

Finally, in the north of the county Chas Ockwell of Cricklade specialised in harvest gloves tanned with alum and salt. The firm was set up by 1867 and occupied a number of buildings, in 1870 the Wesleyan Chapel, and in 1933 the Town Hall. In the present century the firm has specialised in the manufacture of industrial gloves.

Paper

Paper making was attracted to Wiltshire in the 16th century by the abundance of water, clear, and with sufficient power to operate the mill machinery. Predominantly located in the north west, on the By Brook, and also in close proximity to Salisbury, the industry moved into former corn and fulling mills.

The earliest paper mill was at Bemerton Mill in West Harnham which was used from 1554 to 1860. In Downton two mills were used for paper making. Both were opposite the tannery on either side of the river. That to the west was used from 1740 and in 1885–1890 Wiggins, Teape, Carter and Barlow used it to produce hand made paper, and when it finally closed after the First World War it was occupied by Mark Palmer and Son, the last of the Downton paper makers. The adjacent mill on the east side of the river, latterly the electricity generating station, was used by the Jellyman family between 1830 and 1860 for the production of paste boards. The mill at Bulford was used between the mid 18th century and about 1880 when it was dismantled. A number of paper makers seem to have used the mill, which was finally used for the manufacture of blotting and filter paper.

In the north east, Calstone Mill on the Marden was advertised in 1791 as a new overshot paper mill. Advantages claimed for the mill at the time, were that the stream was the best for writing paper, that rags were available locally (probably from woollen mills) and that it was the first mill on the stream. In 1876 the mill was last recorded as being owned by William John Dowding and Sons.

The greatest concentration of paper mills in the county was on the By Brook; paper was made at Long Dean (Yatton Keynell), Widdenham and Doncombe Mills (Colerne), Weavern Mill (Biddestone) and Rag Mill and Chaps Mill (Slaughterford). These latter mills were the last survival of the Wiltshire paper industry; though Rag Mill is now derelict, Chaps Mill is still in operation under the ownership of Messrs. W. J. Dowding & Sons.

The Rag Mill which provided 'stuff', made from rags, to the main mill was powered by a 2.77 m (9 ft) wide water wheel supplemented by a gas engine. Power was transmitted by shaft and pulley to the machinery which consisted of two rag cutting machines, one of which was a simple chaff cutter, the other a purpose made rag cutter; the rags were transported by conveyor belt to the rag boilers, agitated by the power drive and finally broken into individual fibres in one of two breaking engines. There was also a pump and grindstone driven off the shaft, the grindstone being used to sharpen the blades of the cutting machines. From the breaking engines the 'stuff' was stored in steep tanks in which the chemicals used in the boilers drained off; from the steep tanks the 'stuff' was transported to Chaps Mill in vats of elm mounted on bogies.

Tobacco

From its introduction to Bristol in the late 16th century, tobacco spread rapidly to the surrounding areas. In the 17th century many farmers in the county found it a more profitable crop than corn. However, in 1675 the Earl of Danby ordered the enforcement of Acts to ban the crop. Trades associated with tobacco flourished, with many firms incorporating pipes in their trade tokens. Amesbury was famed for its clay pipe manufacture, while in Devizes one of the earliest snuff factories in the country was that of E. & W. Anstie Ltd.

In the early days of snuff production a windmill

supplemented by a donkey wheel was used for grinding, but as trade increased water-mills were used at Poulshot, Calstone and Whistley; in the 18th century windmills on the ruins of Devizes Castle were also used. In 1830 a 10 h.p. Boulton and Watt steam engine was purchased for £700 from Haden's of Trowbridge. About the same time Paul Anstie devised what is said to be the first tobacco cutting machine; the firm produced fine shag tobaccos and following the Crimean War, cigarettes. In 1944 the firm was purchased by the Imperial Tobacco Company and closed in 1960. The snuff mill from Anstie's factory is now in the Bristol City Museum.

In Bradford-on-Avon a small mill suffering from the decline in the cloth trade started to grind snuff. An accident at the end of the 18th century gave the town the soubriquet of 'Snuffy Bradford'.

In 1910 the prohibition on tobacco growing was lifted and satisfactory crops were produced in Whaddon, the Teffonts and Dinton. These were taken by H. Stevens & Co. of Salisbury where the firm had been established since about 1780. The firm operated from Silver Street, where from 1865 all the manufacturing was carried out at the Town Mill.

In the present century Imperial Tobacco opened a factory in Westbury to accommodate their Shoreditch works, while in Swindon a large factory was opened in Colbourne Street, by W. D. & H. O. Wills.

Stratton St. Margaret: The Kingsdown Brewery is the oldest brewery still in use in Wiltshire

Westbury Leigh: The Maltings

Devizes: A corner of the cutting room in the former Snuff & Tobacco Factory. (Photo., Devizes Museum)

Devizes: The former Central Wiltshire Bacon Factory, now occupied by Cross Engineering Ltd.

8. TROWBRIDGE SITES

Trowbridge is a town particularly rich in surviving industrial sites. Presented here is a selection of them. Since it would have been possible to give an almost unlimited list of sites associated with the textile trade those which are included are only a representative selection.

TEXTILE INDUSTRY

Clothiers' Houses

1. The Parade
2. Lloyds Bank
3. Courtfield House

Factories

Steam/Water

4. Stone Mill

Steam

5. Brick Mill
6. Castle Mill
7. Ashton Mill
8. Studley Mill
9. Innox Mill
10. Home Mill (still in use)

Weaving Sheds

11. Ashton Mill

Hand Loom Shops

12. Yerbury Street
13. Newtown

Wool Drying Stoves

14. Ashton Mill

Handle Houses

15. River Biss

Office Blocks

16. Studley Mill
17. 4–5 Fore Street

OTHER SITES

18 and 19. West Ashton Road, site of toll house

20. Stallard Street, site of toll house
21. Roundstone Street milestone
22. Trowbridge Railway Station and goods shed
23. Trowbridge Museum
24. Silver Street Foundry
25. St. George's Foundry
26. Shailes Lane Foundry (Roberts & Morris)
27. Usher's (Watney's) Brewery
28. Usher's (Watney's) Maltings

TROWBRIDGE: textiles and other industrial buildings

textiles buildings ▒ other industrial buildings ▥

9. MUSEUMS IN WILTSHIRE WITH INDUSTRIAL ARCHAEOLOGICAL CONTENT

Wiltshire Archaeological & Natural History Society Museum, Long Street, Devizes.
Salisbury & South Wiltshire Museum, St. Ann Street, Salisbury
Borough of Thamesdown Museums & Art Gallery, Museum & Art Gallery, Bath Road, Swindon
  Great Western Railway Museum, Faringdon Road, Swindon
  Richard Jefferies Museum, Coate Water, Swindon
Athelstan Museum, Gloucester Road, Malmesbury
Yelde Hall Museum, Chippenham
Lackham Agricultural Museum, Lackham College, nr. Chippenham
Trowbridge Museum, Civic Hall, Trowbridge
Fox Talbot Museum, Lacock, nr. Chippenham

10. INDUSTRIAL ARCHAEOLOGICAL SOCIETIES IN WILTSHIRE

Wiltshire Archaeological & Natural History Society, The Museum, Long Street, Devizes
South Wiltshire Industrial Archaeological Society, Hon. Secretary, D. Davies, Esq., 22 Minster Street, Salisbury
West Wiltshire Industrial Archaeological Society, Hon. Secretary, J. Sawtell, Esq., Hope Cottage, Station Road, Holt, nr. Trowbridge
Swindon Archaeological Society, Hon. Secretary, M. Stone, Esq., 25 Bute Close, Highworth, Swindon

11. SELECT BIBLIOGRAPHY

General Works

BODEY, H., Discovering industrial archaeology and history. 1975

BRACEGIRDLE, B., The archaeology of the Industrial Revolution. 1973

BUCHANAN, R. A., Industrial archaeology in Britain. 1972

BURTON, A., Remains of a revolution. 1975

COSSONS, N., The B. P. book of industrial archaeology. 1975

COSSONS, N. and HUDSON, K., Industrial archaeologist's guide, 1969–70. 1969

HUDSON, K., The archaeology of industry. 1976

HUDSON, K., Handbook for industrial archaeologists; a guide to fieldwork and research. 1967

HUDSON, K., Industrial archaeology; a new introduction. 3rd ed. 1976

HUDSON, K., The industrial archaeology of southern England. 2nd ed. 1968

HUDSON, K., A pocket book for industrial archaeologists. 1976

MAJOR, J. K., Fieldwork in industrial archaeology. 1975.

PANNELL, J. P. M., The techniques of industrial archaeology. 2nd ed. 1974

SIMMONS, J., Transport museums. 1970

THE VICTORIA HISTORY OF WILTSHIRE, Volume 4. 1959

Roads

BAKER, M., Discovering the westward stage. 1972

COCHRANE, C., The lost roads of Wessex. 1969

CROSS, D. A. E., The development of traffic signs. *Industrial Archaeology*, 1968 5(3), 266–72

FARRANT, J. P., Scout Motors of Salisbury; a history of the motor engineering firm, 1902–21. 1967

HAYNES, R. I. E., Wiltshire milestones. *In:* WILTSHIRE COUNTY COUNCIL. Leisure in Wiltshire. 2nd ed. 1968. 52–57

JERVOISE, E., Ancient bridges of the south of England. 1930

MARGARY, I., Roman roads in Britain. Volume I. South of The Fosse Way–Bristol Channel. 1955

MORLAND, T. E., The great western postroad. *Wiltshire Industrial Archaeology*, 1970. 2, 26–27

MORLAND, T. E., Second hand milestones. *Wiltshire Industrial Archaeology*, 1969. 1, 8–9

MORLAND, T. E., Two Wessex roadways. *Wiltshire Industrial Archaeology*, 1974. 5, 30–34

PAWSON, E., Transport and economy; the turnpike roads of eighteenth century Britain. 1977

ROBERTS, C., And so to Bath. 1940

TIMPERLEY, H. W. and BRILL, E., Ancient trackways of Wessex. 1965

Canals—General Works

ATTERBURY, P. and DARWIN, A. *eds*. Nicholson's guides to the waterways. Vol. 3, South West. 1973

DE MARE, E., The canals of England. 1950

GLADWIN, D. D., Victorian and Edwardian canals from old photographs. 1976

HADFIELD, C., British canals; an illustrated history. 5th ed. 1974

HADFIELD C., The canal age. 1968

HADFIELD, C., The canals of southern England. 1955

METCALFE, L. and VINCE, J., Discovering canals; a guide for the motorist. 3rd ed. 1975

RANSOM, P. J. G., Waterways restored. 1974

ROLT, L. T. C., The inland waterways of England. 1950

ROLT, L. T. C., Navigable waterways. 1969

RUSSELL, R., Discovering lost canals. 1975

RUSSELL, R., The lost canals of England and Wales. 1971

Canals—Kennet and Avon

CLEW, K. R., The Kennet and Avon Canal. 2nd ed. 1973

CLEW, K. R., The Kennet and Avon Canal guide No. 1—Historical background. 1974

HAMMOND, N., The Kennet and Avon Waterway. The complete chart, western half, parts 1 to 4, Avonmouth to All Cannings. 1969

REBUILDING A WOOD CRANE. *Industrial Archaeology*, 1973. 10(3), 335

SMITH, C. H., Through the Kennet and Avon Canal by motorboat. 1929

Canals—Salisbury

BRAUN, H., The Salisbury Canal; a Georgian misadventure. *Wiltshire Archaeological Magazine* 1962. 58, 171–80

CROSS, D. A. E., The Salisbury Avon Navigation. *Industrial Archaeology*, 1970. 7(2), 121–30

CROSS, D. A. E., The Salisbury Avon Navigation. *Wiltshire Archaeological Magazine*, 1970. 65, 172–6

WELCH, E., The bankrupt canal; Southampton and Salisbury, 1795–1808. 1966

Canals—Thames and Severn

HOUSEHOLD, H., The Thames and Severn Canal. 1969

VINER, D. J., The Thames and Severn Canal; a survey from historical photographs. 1976

Canals—Other

CLEW, K. R., The Somersetshire Coal Canal and Railway. 1970

DALBY, L. J., The Wilts and Berks Canal. 1971

Railways—General Works

CASSERLEY, H. C., Wessex. 1975. (Railway history in pictures series)

CROSS, D. A. E., Narrow gauge railway on Salisbury Plain. *Industrial Archaeology* 1970. 7(4), 465–6

ELTON, *Sir* A., The prehistory of railways with special reference to the early quarry railways of North Somerset. *Proceedings of the Somersetshire Archaeological and Natural History Society*, 1963, 107, 31–59

FARRANT, J., A railroad to Salisbury; the proposal of .1834. *Wiltshire Industrial Archaeology*, 1969. 1, 10–13

GREVILLE, M. D. and SPENCE, J., Closed passenger lines of Great Britain. 1827–1947. Rev. ed. 1974

HUDSON, K., The early years of the railway community in Swindon. *Transport History*, 1968. 1(2), 130–52

HUDSON, K., Working to rule; railway workshop rules, a study of industrial discipline. 1970

SAWTELL, J. C., 34002 Salisbury. *Wiltshire Industrial Archaeology*, 1969. 1, 30–33

THODY, D. W. J., Railway reveries. *Wiltshire Industrial Archaeology*, 1974. 5, 35–40

THOMAS, D. St. J., The West Country. Rev. ed. 1966. (Regional history of the railways of the British Isles, 1).

VOCE, A. P., The Murhill tramroad. *Wiltshire Industrial Archaeology*, 1969. 1, 14–19

WILLIAMS, A., Life in a railway factory. 1915

WILLIAMS, P., Britain's railway museums. 1974

Railways—Great Western

BOURNE, J. C., History and description of the Great Western Railway. 1846. (1969 reprint)

BRITISH RAIL, WESTERN REGION 'Western Enterprise' a celebration in pictures and words of the Western class 2,700 h.p. diesel hydraulic locomotives . . . 1975

EVERSLEY, D. E. C., The Great Western Railway and the Swindon Works in the great depression. *University of Birmingham Historical Journal*, 1957. 5(2), 167–90

GREAT WESTERN PROGRESS. 1835-1935. 1935 (1972 reprint)

GREAT WESTERN RAILWAY, The town and works of Swindon with a brief history of the Broad Gauge. 1892

HOLT MAGAZINE, Holt Junction: the story of a village railway station, based upon research by many persons and information from many sources. 1966

MACDERMOT, E. T., History of the Great Western Railway. 2nd rev. ed. 2 vols. 1964 (1973 reprint)

NOCK, O. S., G.W.R. steam. 1972

NOCK, O. S., Great Western Railway; an appreciation. 1951

NOCK, O. S., The Great Western Railway in the 19th century. 1962

NOCK, O. S., The Great Western Railway in the 20th century. 1964

ROLT, L. T. C., The Great Western Railway Museum, Swindon. 1963

TANNER, G. H. J., The Calne Branch. 1972

VAUGHAN, A., A pictorial record of Great Western signalling. 1973

Railways—London and South Western

ELLIS, C. H., The South Western Railway; its mechanical history and background 1838–1922. 1956

NOCK, O. S., The London and South Western Railway. 1965 (1972 reprint)

Railways—Midland and South Western Junction

MAGGS, C. G., The Midland and South Western Junction Railway. 1967

SANDS, T. B., The Midland and South Western Junction Railway. 1959

Power

ARMFIELD, J. H., The craft of mill-gearing. *Industrial Archaeology*, 1972. 9(3) 296–300

BRUNNER, H. and MAJOR, J. K., Water raising by animal power. *Industrial Archaeology*, 1972. 9(2) 117–151

CROFTON PUMPING ENGINES. *Industrial Archaeology*, 1968. 5(4), 415–6

CROSS, D. A. E., Hydro-electricity from the Salisbury Avon and tributaries. *Wiltshire Industrial Archeaology*, 1969. 1, 26–29

CROSS, D. A. E., Hydro-electricity from the Salisbury Avon and tributaries. *Wiltshire Industrial Archaeology*, 1972/3. 4, 24–29

CROSS, D. A. E., Preserving a Wiltshire windmill. *Industrial Archaeology*, 1972. 9(3) 315

KENNET AND AVON CANAL TRUST, Crofton pump. 1971

NICHOLSON, R. P. de B., Two Wiltshire watermills. *Wiltshire Industrial Archaeology*, 1971. 3, 21–29

REYNOLDS, J., Windmills and watermills. 1970

SAWTELL, J. C., Institutional steam power. *Wiltshire Industrial Archaeology*, 1970. 2, 18–25

TANN, J., The employment of power in the West of England wool textile industry 1790–1840. *In:* HARTE, N. B. and PONTING, K. G. *eds.* Textile history and economic history; essays in honour of Miss Julia de Lacy Mann. 1973, 196–224

WILLOUGHBY, R. W. H., Watermills in West Wiltshire. *Wiltshire Archaeological Magazine*, 1969. 64, 71–99

Quarries

BATH STONE, *The Builder*, 1895. 68, 273–8, 291–5

BOX HILL AND ITS BATH STONE QUARRIES, *The Builder*, 1862. 20, 613–6

COTHAM CAVING GROUP, Box freestone mines, Wiltshire. 1967

HUDSON, K., The fashionable stone. 1971

HUGGINS, G. M., Bath Stone: a short history. 1976

PICTOR & SONS, Bath Stone quarries, Box. 1883

RANDALL, J., Bath freestone. *The Builder*, Oct. 1, 1864, p. 719–721

TUCKER, R. J., Box quarries, Wiltshire, *Industrial Archaeology*, 1968. 5(2), 178–83

TUCKER, R. J., Scripta legenda (Box Quarries, Wiltshire) Volume 1—Lower Hill Series. 1976

TUCKER, R. J., Some notable Wiltshire quarrymen. 1973

Textiles

BECKINSALE, R. P. *ed.*, The Trowbridge woollen industry as illustrated by the stock books of John and Thomas Clark. 1804–1824. 1951

MANN, J. de L., The cloth industry in the West of England from 1640 to 1880. 1971

MANN, J. de L., Clothiers and weavers in Wiltshire during the eighteenth century. *In:* PRESSNELL, L. S. *ed.*, Studies in the Industrial Revolution; presented to T. S. Ashton. 1960

MANN, J. de L., Documents illustrating the Wiltshire textile trades in the eighteenth century. 1964

MANN, J. de L., A Wiltshire family of clothiers: George and Hester Wansey, 1683–1714. *Economic History Review*, 1956–7. 2nd series, 9, 241–53

RAMSAY, G. D., The Wiltshire woollen industry in the sixteenth and seventeenth centuries. 1943

PONTING, K. G., Clothiers' pattern books. *Industrial Archaeology*, 1965. 2(4), 147–9

PONTING, K. G., A history of the West of England cloth industry. 1957

PONTING, K. G., The structure of the Somerset-Wiltshire border woollen industry 1816–40. *In:* HARTE, N. B. and PONTING, K. G. *eds.*, Textile history and economic history: essays in honour of Miss Julia de Lacy Mann. 1973, 163–195

PONTING, K. G., The woollen industry of South-West England. 1971

ROGERS, K. H., Trowbridge clothiers and their houses, 1660–1800. *In:* HARTE, N. B. and PONTING, K. G. *eds.* Textile history and economic history; essays in honour of Miss Julia de Lacy Mann. 1973, 138–62

ROGERS, K. H., Wiltshire and Somerset woollen mills. 1976

Agriculture

AUBREY, John, Natural history of Wiltshire; edited by John Britton. 1847 (1969 reprint)

BETTEY, J. H., Rural life in Wessex, 1500–1900. 1977

BOWEN, H. C., Ancient fields; a tentative analysis of vanishing earthworks and landscapes. 1961

BOWEN, H. C. and FOWLER, P. J., Romano-British rural settlement in Dorset and Wiltshire. *In:* Rural settlement in Roman Britain; papers given at a C.B.A. Conference 1965, edited by Charles Thomas, 1966. 43–67

CHAMBERS, J. D. and MINGAY, G. E., The agricultural revolution, 1750–1880. 1966

COBBETT, W., Rural rides. 1830. Everyman Edition, 1948

DARBY, H. C. and FINN, R. W., The Domesday geography of South-West England. 1967

DAVIS, T., General view of the agriculture of Wiltshire. 1794

DEFOE, D., A tour through England and Wales. Everyman Edition. 1927

FINBERG, H. P. R. *ed.*, The agrarian history of England and Wales; volume 4, 1500–1640 edited by Joan Thirsk. 1967

HUDSON, K., The Bath and West: a bicentenary history. 1976

KERRIDGE, E., The floating of the Wiltshire water-meadows. *Wiltshire Archaeological Magazine*, 1953–4. 55, 107–118

KERRIDGE, E., The note book of a Wiltshire farmer in the early seventeenth century. *Wiltshire Archaeological Magazine*, 1951–2, 54, 416–28

KERRIDGE, E., The sheepfold in Wiltshire and the floating of the watermeadows. *Economic History Review*, 1953–4 2nd series, 6, 282–9

TAYLOR, C. C., Fields in the English landscape. 1975

Miscellaneous

BRISTOW, H. R., The village genius; William Lander, brazier of Mere. *Wiltshire Industrial Archaeology*, 1971. 3, 9–17

CAREY, G., The whole of Malmesbury. *Industrial Archaeology*, 1965. 2(4), 172–5

ELKINS, P., The Iron Duke. *Wiltshire Industrial Archaeology*, 1970, 2, 16–17

GOODHUGH, P. S., Marconi on Salisbury Plain. *Wiltshire Industrial Archaeology*, 1974. 5, 26–29

GOODHUGH, P. S The Poor Law in Amesbury. *Wiltshire Industrial Archaeology*, 1970. 2, 5–12

MAJOR, J. K., A survival of the Wiltshire paper industry. *Industrial Archaeology*, 1964. 1(1) 17–20

MAJOR, J. K., The windmills of John Wallis Titt. 1977

MOORE, C. N., The Salisbury cutler industry. *Wiltshire Industrial Archaeology*, 1972/3. 4, 7–13

MOORE, C. N., Salisbury gunsmiths. *Wiltshire Industrial Archaeology*, 1972/3. 4, 21–23

MOORE, C. N., Salisbury pewterers. *Wiltshire Industrial Archaeology*, 1972/3. 4, 30–31

MOORE, N., Cast iron monuments. *Wiltshire Industrial Archaeology*, 1969. 1, 25

MOORE, N., Wiltshire brown ware. *Wiltshire Industrial Archaeology*, 1969. 1, 34

RICHARDSON, A., Salisbury cinemas. *Wiltshire Industrial Archaeology*, 1974. 5, 13–18

WATTS, J., A history of Salisbury water works. *Wiltshire Industrial Archaeology*, 1972/3. 4, 14–20

WATTS, J., Salisbury and Winchester sewage works. *Wiltshire Industrial Archaeology*, 1974. 5, 19–25